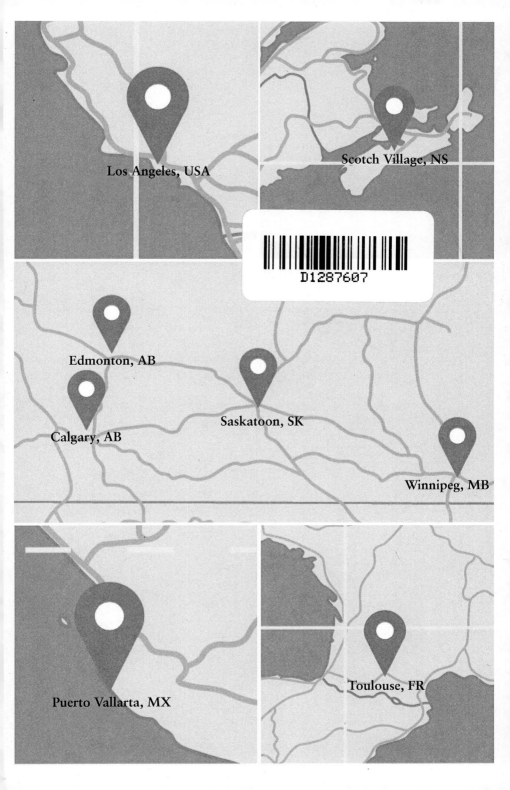

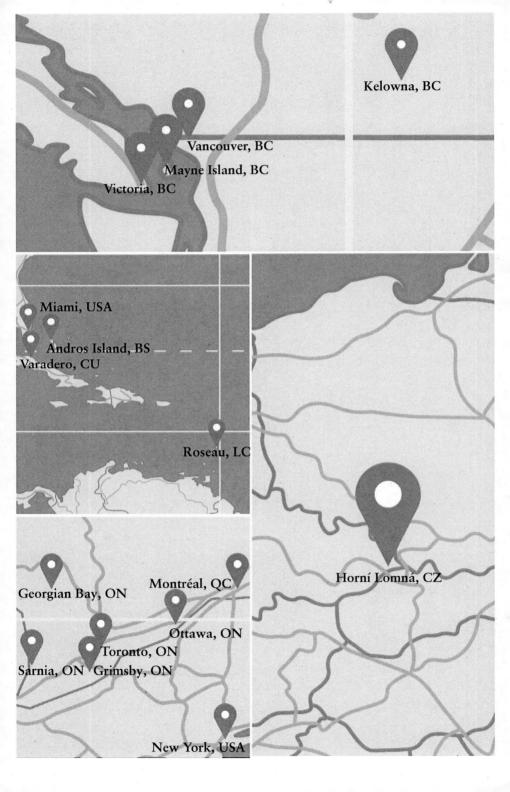

LOCATIONS OF GRIEF

LOCATIONS OF GRIEF

an emotional geography

24 PERSONAL ESSAYS
EDITED BY CATHERINE OWEN

WOLSAK
& WYNN

Cover and interior design: Jennifer Rawlinson
Cover image: Sharon Wish
Typeset in Sabon LT Pro and Minion Pro
Printed by Brant Service Press in Brantford
Printed on certified 100% post-consumer Rolland Enviro Paper

The lyric on page 30 is from the song "Night Drive" written by Garnet Rogers, published by Snow Goose Songs Canada, (SOCAN).
The lyrics excerpted on pages 130–31 are from the song "Love Is All" written by Kristian Matsson, published by Rough Trade Publishing.
All lyrics reproduced with permission.

The publisher gratefully acknowledges the support of the Ontario Arts Council, the Canada Council for the Arts and the Government of Canada.

Wolsak & Wynn
280 James Street North
Hamilton, ON
Canada L8R 2L3

Library and Archives Canada Cataloguing in Publication

Title: Locations of grief : an emotional geography : twenty-four personal essays / edited by Catherine Owen.
Names: Owen, Catherine, 1971- editor.
Identifiers: Canadiana 20200177958 | ISBN 9781989496145 (softcover)
Subjects: LCSH: Grief in literature. | CSH: Canadian essays (English)—21st century. | LCGFT: Essays.
Classification: LCC PS8367.G75 L63 2020 | DDC C814/.6080353—dc23

American literature is about grief
spread over space.
– Richard Harrison

Grief is wild; it's a feral energy.
– Francis Weller

CONTENTS

FIVE: FOREIGN REALMS

PREFACE, OR
A PLACE FROM WHICH TO BEGIN

Catherine Owen

I started thinking about the relationship between landscape and grieving even before he died. As with much knowledge, it came to me through poetry. The sonnet "Time Does Not Bring Relief" by Edna St. Vincent Millay ends with the lines:

> And entering with relief some quiet place
> Where never fell his foot or shone his face
> I say, "There is no memory of him here!"
> And so stand stricken, so remembering him.

In the weeks and then months following Chris's death, I would recite these lines many times to myself, comprehending ever more deeply the bond between loss and place, mourning and intimate spaces, land and memory. And how the ghost of the loved person in your mind begins to reshape realms they never even inhabited so that, for a period of years, everywhere one goes is altered, changed, re-topographied in a sense by their phantom status.

I also began to pay attention to how often place is referenced in grief texts – those "eulogized spaces" as Gaston Bachelard calls them, a library I started to accumulate, featuring titles from C.S. Lewis to Joan Didion, Roland Barthes to Neil Peart. Lewis, in *A Grief Observed*, recounts how, initially, it is hard to revisit places marked by a lost beloved but that, eventually, absence is "like the sky, spread over everything." Peart, in *Ghost Rider*, embraces travel as a mode through which to detach himself from the constant reminders of his deceased wife and daughter in places as disparate as their cabin in Lac St. Brutus, Quebec, and the corner of Bay and Bloor in Toronto, while Barthes grows to loathe travel after his mother's death because it takes him away from the familiar "locality of the room" where she took her final breaths. Didion, in her memoir *A Year of Magical Thinking*, describes grief itself as a tangible yet mysterious place "none of us know until we reach it," a sentiment Don Coles echoes in one of his poems where one literally "come[s] to grief," rounding a "corner and there it is, you have / come to it." In more theoretical fashion, Priscila Uppal in *We Are What We Mourn* depicts landscape in elegy as an "active site for reconnection with the dead," and a tome on the prevalence of the roadside shrine in BC called *Public Grief, Private Mourning* focuses on how, as we have become gradually dislocated from rural and stable communities, we seek to transform a variety of landscapes into places for remembering, including such virtual locales as Facebook pages. Grief is everywhere in the land, the very soil steeped in it, the air around it imbued with loss. This reality should be taken as both marking the difficulty inherent in mourning, its inescapability, but also as normalizing the process of grieving: it does not occur in tidy stages or certain places; it is wherever we are and, in some sense, always.

Locations of Grief: An Emotional Geography draws together twenty-four Canadian writers of a range of ages, ethnicities and gender identities. One is primarily a well-known painter. One writes about the death of her dog; another about the strangely moving suicide of a stranger. Most, however, speak about the deaths of intimately known individuals from causes as diverse as cancer and drowning to car accidents and overdoses. Some write about local landscapes, such as their back garden in Ontario; others recall locations where loss occurred, some as far-flung as Saint Lucia, New York and the Bahamas.

The anthology attends to what Bachelard called a "topoanalysis," or a study, in memoir form, of the intimate sites of our lives. Divided into five sections, each features a unifying location, a particular geographical locus forever altered by the experience of death. Although some pieces fall into several categories, my aim was to focus on the memoir's overarching landscape: the primary room, country or natural feature eternally impacted by loss so that the writer wishes to vacate the area or more deeply attach themselves to the realm, or perhaps wherever they flee a haunted sense of the region, topography or element pursues them.

Part one is "The Garden." Alice Major commemorates her dog's favourite space, the yard, and in the process examines the humanized nature of elegy; David Haskins buries his wife's ashes in this most familiar place; Lynn Tait plants a tree for her son; and Jenna Butler commemorates her lost daughters on her farm. In part two, "The Neighbourhood," six writers depict how their wider environs shift in meaning once they directly suffer a death. Steven Heighton's loss may have been of a stranger, but being witness to the aftermath of a neighbour's suicide nonetheless produced a grief of incomprehension that turned him, for a time, into a geographical detective, obsessed with the landscape features that signified, or prefigured, this man's tragedy. Alice Burdick, Onjana Yawnghwe and Marilyn Dumont detail the varying ways an urban neighbourhood transmogrifies following a death, and Katherine Bitney and Sharon Thesen attend to more rural/suburban permutations of grief.

The third section, "Elemental Spaces," though the featured landscapes may be urban or rural, in proximity to home or at a distance, pay homage to the matter of the ecosystem: water, as with Waubgeshig Rice, Canisia Lubrin, Christine Lowther and Nikki Reimer, in scenes of, respectively, recollection, tragedy, detachment and burial; and rock, commemorated in Catherine Graham's quarry, as a place of thwarted healing and solace.

Part four then features the unfortunate but also often necessary "Clinical Zones," both hospitals and funeral/cremation homes. Richard Harrison's mother chooses to die in a hospice by lethal injection; Catherine Greenwood's father takes his final breaths in an Alzheimer's ward in a state of disorientation. And I myself must cope with the cold regulations of the coroner's office and Simply Cremations, where rules establish walls between the survivor and the deceased, their procedures inevitably leaking into the surrounding landscapes, increasing my own detachment from the loci of loss.

The final section, "Foreign Realms," features writers dealing with deaths far from home or while they are away, from Jane Eaton Hamilton's Bahamas to James Picard's New York and Lisa Richter's sojourns in the Caribbean and Montreal. Daniel Zomparelli experiences his sister's and later his mother's deaths as a source of disorientation between locales that serves to increase his fear of travel, though eventually encourages him to relocate to Los Angeles, while the death of her father leads Theresa Kishkan to re-examine her family's history in the Czech Republic. In closing, the unexpected loss of Ben Gallagher's girlfriend sends him back to Scotch Village, Nova Scotia, from Hamilton, Ontario, in an attempt to preserve his loved mate's legacy and to honour her final wishes.

Locations of Grief: An Emotional Geography is an act of what the Welsh call "hiraeth" or, in essence, a commemoration of the "homesick grief for the lost places of your past." This kind of grief particularly relates to how death creates or deepens a sense of homesickness, establishing a new relationship with the world as something transient, shifting, scarred. Or even, sometimes, making it more beloved, the locus of memory becoming, in its present, an ineffable realm of longing.

WORKS CITED

Barthes, Roland. *A Mourner's Diary*. New York: Hill & Wang, 2009.

Didion, Joan. *The Year of Magical Thinking*. New York: Alfred A. Knopf, 2005.

Maté, Gabor. *In the Realm of Hungry Ghosts: Close Encounters with Addiction*. Toronto: Vintage, 2009.

Oates, Joyce Carol. *A Widow's Story: A Memoir*. New York: Harper Collins, 2011.

Van Gennep, Arnold. *The Rites of Passage*. Moscow: University of Idaho, 1909.

ONE:
THE GARDEN

WE HAVE ELEGIES TO WRITE

Alice Major

I am mourning the dog.

Just a little dog, one of the thousands that bark and scamper in our urban off-leash parks, a blur of brown and tan, caramel and black. Almost indistinguishable – you are sometimes reduced to looking for a familiar pink harness or plaid coat to tell whether that's Georgia or Gus, Maggie, Princess or Whiffle.

But you always know your own little dog from all the others. Whiffle's soft poodle-droopy ears, the squared-off shape from the terrier side of her mixed breed, her gait with its distinctive hop, the frill of white edging her forepaws. Although my brain's recognition systems are specialized for human faces, I'd never mistake her for any other dog. Nor would she have mistaken me for any other two-legged, parka-clad creature strolling on the path.

This would have been exactly the right day for the park – cool and gold. Instead, I'm indoors without her, looking at the tangle of bushes and branches beyond my window. Three weeks ago, it was an indistinguishable blur of green.

Now autumn is starting to make its distinctions: the butter-yellow of ash leaves, the pinkish-tan of flowering almond. My thoughts this afternoon are as entangled as the branches: What makes us distinct, completely identifiable as "us"? What about that old idea of a "soul" that marks us apart from everyone else? Do animals have souls?

On that last question, religion is dubious. "Soul" is a status that is, in Christian traditions anyway, particularly human. Science is dubious about the concept altogether – at least about the kind of immaterial, immortal soul that isn't connected to physical meat and neurons. Still, in different ways, religion and science can agree there's something that makes both the dog and I each unique and irreplaceable.

Meanwhile, I am missing that little dog who chased squirrels in the garden beyond this window until just a few days ago. As I stare through the glass, a faint breeze stirs a single leaf on the tip of a branch. Its serrated edges stand out clearly in this afternoon light that is calm, attentive, elegiac.

Elegy. It is one of the essential wellsprings of poetry, swelling out of our deep need to pay attention to the loss of someone loved, to give meaning to their life.

The word itself comes from a particular form used in ancient Greek literature, using a particular pattern of stresses. This strict pattern could be used for any number of subjects – war and love were as appropriate as mourning. Over the centuries, poetry in English came to flip these requirements. Instead of referring to a specific form used for a variety of subjects, "elegy" became a poem that could take any form the poet cared to use, but which focused on very specific content.

Someone is dead, and we need to come to terms with it.

*

But really now – writing an elegy for the dog? I feel frustrated with myself, snivelling here at the window. I'm in the rut of old guilt about having my heart clamped so firmly around one small animal when the world needs so much care and attention. "What are you doing for the refugees, Alice?" I ask myself sternly, knowing that the answer is "Damn all."

Then I bow my head and acknowledge that this is how love works. We're like Lego blocks, designed to fit together with immediate neighbours, and through that process, connecting with more distant blocks in order to build houses and towers. I can/should do things for refugees, but there is no way that I can mourn their individual suffering as I can constantly miss the presence of my immediate companions.

And, after all, isn't it anthropocentric to say that animals aren't worth loving in the same way that we love people? Their lives are as whole and complete; they are not "lesser beings" to themselves. Would I really be a better person if I didn't care as much? In fact, I'd probably be less human. I know that what I feel for Whiffle comes out the evolutionary kit bag that disposes us to care greatly for small children, that swell of adult-to-infant love. It's a capacity that all mammals have. However, humans succeeded in large measure because we were especially good at embracing that emotion and extending it – not just our own children but others; not just members of our own tribe but others; and ultimately, not just our own species but others.

I do worry, though, that love for an animal is like one of those finishing-off blocks supplied in Lego kits, the half-length ones that tidy up the end of a row. The love of a child goes on to connect with others in the world, but the pet will not go off to click into other networks in your absence. The love of an animal does come back to us, but it *is* a bit self-indulgent; it doesn't spur me on the way that caring for a child or grandchild would connect me with a larger world, a future time.

That need for connection to the larger world lies at the heart of elegy. An elegy doesn't necessarily tell you the colour of the loved one's eyes, the small details of their dress – these are the content of personal lyric. Nor is elegy the same as dirge or threnody, the words that pour from new grief. Elegies are less intense yet larger in other ways. They are attempts to find meaning, to place the departed life in context. In classic elegies, the natural world joins in the mourning, often in opposition to the cruelty or indifference of human society.

One of the big, emblematic elegies in English literature is Walt Whitman's "When Lilacs Last in the Dooryard Bloom'd," about the death of Abraham Lincoln. Even though the president's name is never mentioned in the poem, he is present as a brilliant evening star setting in the west. There is the coffin that journeys by day and night, the hermit thrush whose notes sink in warning then burst again in joy, the lilacs that have returned with their fragrance. We wouldn't learn very much from the poem about its political context or the shape of Lincoln's face. We do learn what that brilliant star meant emotionally to the author. We do see Whitman's struggle to find meaning in great national loss.

Little dogs don't matter much to the political dramas of a bigger world. For me, however, Whiffle was more than a child substitute or an emotional bottle stopper, and she did connect me to others; through her death, I'm also mourning my parents.

The dog arrived in our house the same spring that my parents came to live with us, no longer able to cope on their own with my mother's health concerns and my father's cognitive decline. My husband had always wanted a dog. I thought, "Well, if I'm quartering two octogenarians on him, maybe I should throw in a puppy."

They were all good for each other. Neighbours called her "the most-walked dog on the street." Dad played tag with her and helped teach her to shake a paw. I could go to meetings and know they kept each other company.

Looking out this window to the tremble of a leaf, I suddenly hear my mother's soft, Scottish-tinted voice. It came from a time near the end of her life, after my father finally had to go into a dementia ward. She said, "Sometimes, when you are out, I talk to Whiffle. I tell her all my troubles."

Today, this memory stops my heart. She said it as if it were part confession, part something to laugh at, to be a little embarrassed about. And yet it was something very important, a kind of plea, a way of saying how lonely she was.

I suppose I returned some light answer at the time. But now, I am picturing Mum on the blue-green couch, Whiffle sitting beside her, head cocked at the voice speaking to her, the same gentle voice that read storybooks to me when I was a little girl. What exactly would the words have been? The voice that uttered them and the bright eyes that watched her face as she spoke, the perked ears, the consciousness – all of this is gone.

Oh, Whiffle, how you would have jumped and wagged your tail, even years after she left us, if Auntie Mary had walked through the door. The picture makes me smile. I imagine such a reunion and the two of you sitting on the blue sofa, waiting for me. It's a crumb of comfort.

But, no matter how many Rainbow Bridge emoticons friends post on Facebook, I can't take that heavenly resurrection seriously. It simply doesn't make sense to me – that picture comes from my past, not from the future.

Humans have been trying to come to terms with the idea of a soul or spirit and an afterlife for as long as we've been conscious of death. The conceptual world of hunter-gatherers was inhabited by spirits that took on the shape of animals and humans as well as non-living things. Animals' spirits persisted after death and had to be placated and respected when the creature was killed. Ancient civilizations went on to imagine many variations of an existence after death. For the classical Greeks, it was an afterlife in a pale underworld where most souls clustered, shadows of their physical selves, while a fortunate few were made incarnate and immortal by the gods.

Meanwhile, ancient philosophers were debating various ideas of selfhood, coming up with variations on two basic concepts. One was dualism: that a spirit can exist separate from the body and survive without it. The other is that the soul is a life principle, an energizer and animator of the physical, but not separable from it – the stance known as "materialism" or "physicalism." Christianity inherited these contrasting strands from Greek and Hebraic thought, and added its own particular twist: insistence on a physical resurrection of an actual body after death – an afterlife that began with Jesus himself and was then extended to all believers.

Over the centuries, the details of resurrection have been subject to intense theological debate. When does it take place? At the end times? What happens to our souls in the meantime? Are they left in some cryogenic sleep, or do they exist in some sort of conscious afterlife? And the inevitable practical considerations – how would exact physical reassembly work? Theologians tied themselves in knots over the assembly instructions, even getting to the point where they concluded that animals would have to disgorge body parts they had devoured. Which led to the thought that the animals themselves would have to be resurrected, too.

Resurrection of the body – the idea that we will be revived after death as uniquely ourselves, with all our memories and emotions intact – is an essential dogma for denominations such as the Catholic Church. Most adherents don't worry too much about the details. God will sort it all out. For now, we tell children, and ourselves, that it will be all right. We will see Nanna or Princess again in Heaven. They are waiting for us there.

But *does* my little dog have a soul? Most early Christian thinkers wouldn't have thought so. In the fourth century, Saint Augustine pointed out that Christ himself sent a whole herd of swine into the sea as a clear message that "to refrain from the killing of animals and of plants is the height of superstition."

A thousand years later, the great theologian Thomas Aquinas held a more nuanced view. Aquinas had been reading the work of Aristotle (who had recently been reintroduced into Western thought via Arab scholars), and he elaborated on the Greek philosopher's concept of three-layered souls. Humans had a vegetative soul, shared with plants, that enabled growth and reproduction; a sensitive soul, capable of perception and movement, that we shared with animals; and finally, a rational soul, capable of reason and ethics, that is peculiar to humans.

However, medieval theologians had to work hard to preserve the idea that animals were not rational. When they observed complex behaviour in non-human creatures, they kept adding other senses – such as estimativa, the judgment needed to avoid danger – to the sensitive side of the soul ledger, in order to keep the line between humans and animals firmly drawn.

Today, science keeps making that theological line ever more blurry with animal studies that demonstrate human-like cognitive processing. A recent one, for instance, used MRI techniques to show that dogs process words using brain systems in a similar way to humans. If I mentioned Whiffle's name in passing, her ears might twitch – the left hemisphere of her brain had distinguished the word. If I shouted other words in enthusiasm or anger, she would have bounced to her feet, because she was processing the emotion in my voice with her right hemisphere. But if I said "Whiffle!" in that bright, we're-going-for-a-walk tone, she would be up and dancing on her hind legs at the door as sound and emotion came together into meaning for her.

Science has also been smudging another age-old line, the dualist one that separates body and soul into two separate kinds of matter. As neuroscientists peer into our brains, they find that many of the functions traditionally assigned to spirit – like will, reason, judgment, self-control – arise from the action of physical circuits in a brain. The space for a separate soul keeps shrinking.

All this neuroscience creates problems for the idea of immortality. What, if anything, can continue without your physical infrastructure and still be uniquely, identifiably you? And in turn, this creates a problem for the idea of resurrection. If there isn't something separate and divine that distinguishes us, then you *really* need the exact reassembly of the physical body in order to bring about continuity of the unique individual.

However, modern physics also kicks in here and makes the possibility of reassembling the physical even more difficult than the old theologians had imagined. All the atoms in our bodies are continually being swapped out. It's not just the sloughing of skin cells or the continual rebuilding of bone. Even our long-lived neurons are not composed of the same atoms they were seven years ago.

I sometimes amuse myself by wondering: What if you could capture all the atoms that have been part of me in a holding tank and then reconfigure them into exactly the same pattern? What would be the real me? This is not a thought experiment that could ever be carried out, not merely because of technical difficulties but for deep theoretical reasons. In fact, you cannot, ever, tag an electron or proton with an identity. This is one essential aspect of quantum theory that hasn't entered popular culture. We really don't *get* how utterly indistinguishable the bits of matter are that make up our world, our physical bodies.

Electrons are not like Lego blocks. You could put a dab of nail polish on a block and keep track of it as it becomes part of a model cabin or is disassembled into a scatter on the floor. An electron, however, has a complete lack of individuality that includes, in Peter Pesic's words, "the complete equality of all observable features. It has no inherent reference to space or time."

This is what our unique selves are made of: bits that are completely and utterly indistinguishable. Which means we'd be endlessly reproducible – Alice and Whiffle over and over again, assembled from molecules of carbon and passing electrons, arranged into identical patterns. A complicated technological challenge, no doubt, but not one that, in principle, requires a unique, divine spark.

Of course, the even bigger technical challenge would be the need to keep those instantaneous assemblages tracking along together through time. It's not enough to have two identical Alices at this moment. For most of us, time is essential to soul. We require continuity from past into future. We want to remember our lives after death, want to go on being the unique individuals that we are before it. We want the dog to recognize us on the far side of the Rainbow Bridge. We feel our soul isn't simply a pattern, a snapshot of our identity, but a rope woven through time. Shorter strands may have been used to spin it, none of which lasts forever, but it is the same rope from end to end.

In other words, we think of the soul as what a physicist might call a "path-dependent system." For such systems, the math gets complicated. If you are working with a path-*in*dependent system, like a flask full of nitrous oxide, you can simplify the counting: there are so many molecules in state X and so many in state Y. In such a situation, you can usefully use averages to describe the system accurately, without worrying whether any given piece is in any particular state at any given time. But if you have to track every single component individually through time, the calculations and memory requirements rapidly become gigantic, even infinite.

This is what we ask of a divine being that can watch every sparrow's fall, which means watching every molecule of every sparrow for its complete life. And we want that watching to be conscious. *"There goes Alice with Whiffle toward the park."*

Which brings me back to elegy. It is part of the memory system that encodes our consciousness of love, retains snapshots of the Lego castles that are now dismantled and scattered. The tradition has continued to evolve – elegies are not written only for the great and the good, but for the small and local. Even for a dog.

In his "Elegy for a Dead Labrador," Lars Gustafsson writes that he and his pet were:

> Two
> of those places where the universe makes a knot
> in itself, short-lived complex structures
> . . . .
> . . . You were a question
> asked of another question, nothing more,
> and neither had the answer to the other.

"Will you get another dog?" friends ask me. Sometimes I think, yes, I will. There are aspects of dogs that are indistinguishable and interchangeable – wagging tails, bright eyes, an enthusiasm for your company, a physical weight at your side or lying on your feet. Sometimes I want to rush out and replace that presence right now. At the same time, I know that no puppy could be a Lego block to fit into this exact space in my heart.

Yesterday afternoon, I had the impulse to pull out a journal from the time when my parents first arrived here. The entries were a tale of frantic coping. How did I pull it off? Trying to write in the interstices of cooking and cleaning, of dealing with my father's increasingly irrational behaviour and equally irrational professional dramas, of finishing freelance projects and house-training.

Clearly, from the journal's pages, I was fond of the little animal in those early days. She was becoming a companion who curled up on my bed on rare evenings when I could retreat upstairs – a frazzled Rapunzel – while Mum and Dad watched television and my husband attended a meeting. But equally clearly, the dog wasn't as important to me as she would become.

I find this curiously comforting – that love doesn't have to have the happy ending at the beginning, that we don't know what will grow from small things or everything the future will bring. Death, of course, but not only death.

I have become more and more convinced that soul – identity – has something to do with energy and with time. It's more than a static pattern, an arrangement of atoms. It's like the kind of energy that preserves a soliton wave through water, interacting with itself and holding together rather than dispersing as most waves do. A soliton maintains its energy even as it leaves behind the water molecules that formed its shape as it passed through.

Some of us expect the soliton wave of our soul will, sooner or later, lose its material energy and dissipate onto a hiss of sand. Others believe there's something about that pattern of energy that can continue through time and beyond it. But we all believe in the reality of a distinct identity, the uniqueness that makes us essentially ourselves and deserves respect and love. And in this respect, I am certain that animals have souls, too.

I am curiously haunted by the dog. I hear her jingle down the stairs. From the corner of my eye, I see her looking around the frame of the office door to find me. I look out this window and, in the movement of a branch, seem to see her lift her head suddenly to listen for that squirrel. I feel intensely that she is somehow the genius of this small place, that she is inseparable from these layered leaves and me.

The breeze has strengthened, the colours foam together, more leaves separate and fall, spinning. "She must be here," I think, again and again each day.

I know my brain and grief are doing this. I remember how, after my mother died, the world seemed wrapped in a hyperreal dimension for weeks and months. Whatever I passed – the palliative care hospital, a café where we had lunch – seemed somehow sharper, more distinct, like one of those old View-Master toys that made images seem even more self-consciously three-dimensional than the world really is. Once, as I walked Whiffle in the park, I had the overwhelming sense that my mother was walking beside me, her head in its little black hat at my shoulder.

"She *is* still with you," friends would say comfortingly. But I know the sense of an invisible companion is a common illusion for brains under stress. Perhaps it truly is a window to a spirit world that gets opened at certain moments. But personally, I think it's just what grief does to us. It's as though our brains are working hard to stamp the individuals we've lost even more distinctly into our memories, because we will need them.

I don't believe in reunions and Rainbow Bridges, or in that divine consciousness watching every sparrow. But I do believe in the utter importance of memory. I believe the universe itself is a system for remembering, that everything is part of this vast and detailed record – the waves of light that come at us from the big bang, the layers of sediment that have fossilized archaic species, and each of us, individually, writing our journals and prayers.

We each have a past to be treasured and marked with significance – that is how identities continue in time. We have elegies to write.

NINE MONTHS IN A GARDEN

David Haskins

My garden did not ask for the ashes of my beloved. Yet they reside here. Deep below the angel's trumpet flowers I saw in Peru when I hiked the Inca Trail in 1994. Deep below the roots of a David Austin Heritage pink climber rose from England, shouldered by splashes of blue South African agapanthus basking in the perfume of an oleander native to Australia. A figure of St. Francis watches over her.

In a garden, one can manage nature, improve on its randomness, import what in far lands grows common but here looks exotic, create colour palettes against a scale of heights, and time blooms to track the light of days. Contemplation follows after one has gotten one's hands dirty, one's knees bruised, one's muscles stretched. A garden appreciates respect. It asks not to be abandoned. It asks for a gardener.

Now it is winter. All but the rose and St. Francis are safely stowed in my house. The garden sleeps. Nine months after she died, I stand at the window looking out at the desolate brown space, my lips pursed, my face wet. I am silently screaming.

Screaming is what you do when you cannot do anything else.

April 21: Journal

Shirl is in hospital. I wake often and check to see she's still breathing. How many more days/nights before it's over? The twenty-second pause between breaths foreshadows the next, until one will be forever, the chest never to rise again, the open mouth no longer a mere imitation of a death mask. Every inhalation sounds like the rasp of metal chair legs scraped across a stone floor, this a devolution from the rattling gurgle emanating from the body's depths the day before. And then near the end, the sandpaper snore is replaced by a sweet vocal sigh to mark each breath with a promise, perhaps, of more time. More symptoms, more drugs, more complications, more decline. More time at any cost. More time. I hear only the sound and none of the intent. Such is the conversation of the dying.

April 23: Journal

Three a.m. The sedative Versed calms the body, but does it rid the panic? Is she still scared? She wished for no heroic measures. Starvation is now part of the process. I suspect the body will feed off itself. I hope it ends soon and hate myself for hoping this.

Group email

My partner of thirty years died this morning about ten a.m. Shirl was seven days away from her fifty-third birthday. The lung cancers were too aggressive to respond to chemo. Knowing there was no hope for improvement or quality of life, she wanted to go.

I stayed with her every night and watched her suffer, and can honestly say that if it had to end, it was well that it ended quickly.

Her remains will be cremated. There will be no funeral.

One anecdote: As I watched her from my chair-bed beside her, she looked at me, this dying lady, and said, "Are you okay?"

May 21: Journal

My son came to till the soil in the bed that will contain her ashes. The result is complete success, the rock-hard clay crumbling under the power of the tines making its extraction easy, and the bottom of the hole churned to receive the first barrow-loads of topsoil, compost and peat moss, which should arrive in the morning. Tomorrow, I shall have to face burying her ashes under a pink rose, the colour of rose that she loved.

I go through the motions of gardening without heart. As I help remove the soil, a mother robin hops at my feet, looking for easy food for her one scruffy baby that stumbles clumsily through the grass. It's not enough.

May 26: Journal

I spilled her ashes into a hole in the centre of the rose bed. It wasn't as hard as I had expected. No identifiable pieces of bone or teeth to shock me, just a grey-white dust stored in a clear plastic bag clasped by a chrome medallion, packed in a cardboard box with a certificate of cremation in a white envelope taped to the top – as if there were a necessary protocol for packaging human remains. Still, the reduction of her body to these handfuls of ash hidden in the ground is a sobering thought.

I must continue to fill the bed while the rain keeps off. The robin watches me, and I toss her a worm. I need even the smallest life to tend. The bird still feeds her young one, which is now atop the fence. Failing to fly, it flutters to the feathery Japanese maple that sways under its minimal weight.

Watching these birds, I am overcome by how considerate Shirl was of me, with so few requirements from me for her own well-being. While I was involved with my heart surgery, she protected me from how seriously ill she was, grasping at hope where there was little or none. At the same time, she knew that death was coming for her and that she would have to meet it alone, despite the fact that I was with her. I knew nothing of her bravery, her struggle, her heroism.

Today I buried her body. Yesterday I gave away her shoes. How tiny her feet were, how classy she looked in her shiny black pumps, a touch of glamour her unpretentious nature had fun with. I hate flushing her out of my life when I want the impossible opposite – I want her back here with me, I want a second chance to love her as I should have.

May 28: Journal

I am unwell, weak, tired, with bouts of disorientation and impaired vision. I feel unsafe without Shirl here. I read that many a survivor dies soon after their partner's death. It just happens.

I need to keep going. I need to learn how to be alone. I'm going outside to be near her.

June 1: Journal

For two weeks, I've been moving four yards of soil to get the mix in the bed right. Every day a cardinal sings high above me in the locust tree. I thank the bird for coming. Or Shirl for sending it. Irrational notions give comfort. It's not a matter of belief so much as need. People make meanings and metaphors, and then behave as though they are sometimes real. When I slipped Shirl's ashes into the deep hole, I did not say any words. She is more likely in the soul of a cardinal than a hole in the ground.

Sometimes time passes as though she is gone away and will return soon. I just have to wait. In such ways do I track both the reasonable and the fanciful. The trick is knowing which is which.

June 12: Journal

I took down the sympathy cards and put them in the card box where I keep all the cards she'd given me since we met. My heart is broken.

June 13: Journal

Some have told me I was lucky to say goodbye to you. I know what they mean, but that was the morning you died. And if I had said what I said on every other morning, "See you later" or "See you soon" or "I'll be back," would you have lived one more day? And if I had not said "Goodbye" the next day, would you have lived one more day after that? And after that? Would you have lived? And would you have gotten well, miraculously, day by day by day? And come home? And would you be beside me now here tonight? And every new night of life? If I had not said "Goodbye" that morning?

June 14: Email to D

I'm trying to tell myself I'm moving forward, but it's pretty bleak. I don't see the point in continuing alone. I don't want a replacement. In our thirty-one years together, neither of us strayed. We knew that we would wreck the best thing either of us ever had, we would bring hurt upon the other, and so we didn't. Nothing extraordinary in this, I know, but I still feel this way, even now she's gone. I couldn't keep her alive if someone else came in. That's an irrational statement. Like talking to a bird.

June 15: Email to A

Today was our anniversary. It began with the cardinal sitting on the back of a chair on the deck, looking through the dining room window at me only a few feet away. It also began with the first pink rose opening on her Heritage rose bush. At times it feels to me as though this alternate private reality of messenger cardinals and message roses is more vital than the world the living move about in. We call and hear each other across the divide. Her rose is watered with my tears; we will not surrender to losing each other. I am not the keeper of her memory but of her merciful spirit.

June 21: Journal

We will watch the Perseid meteors streak through the locust branches while we lie together in the garden, blathering endlessly into the night until we both fall asleep, exhausted by each other's silly jokes and tongue twisters. How far flung would a flat rat fling if a flat rat could be flung? How we laughed, long and often, and how you kept me feeling young. Stopped now, like someone turned out the lights, emptied the theatre and forgot me. If you die, then so do I. If you live, I live. The world is your vessel. Stay. Now that you are gone everywhere, stay.

August 12: Email to M & H

Tonight, I went next door to use my neighbour's phone. I saw his pictures displayed where he would see them every day, of his deceased wife and her daughter, who had committed suicide. In our vain attempt to keep them with us, our loved ones become photographs, stopped in time. These are what Joan Didion calls "the relentless succession of moments during which we will confront the experience of meaninglessness itself."

August 18: Journal

That moment, when you know you're going to die and you want to live, and there's nothing you can do, you look at me, and you're crying, and you say, I don't want to die. There's panic and fear in the furrows above your eyes, beseeching me to save you from this untimely death. Helpless too, I say, I don't want you to die. And we both know that you will die anyway, that what we want or don't want doesn't matter anymore, that the cancer keeps on eating you up. No, love does not conquer all. Not all. Not this.

Last Days (your words)

When do I get to go home?
Am I expecting too much?
Will it be happening tonight?
I don't want to die like this.
Don't make me cry.
(*waves to me*) In case I don't see you.

September 2: Email to J & P

By the time of the gritLIT literary festival in early April, Shirl had had her first chemo. She was living with excruciating pain in her rib cage, which she attributed to a fractured rib caused by severe coughing. She'd been sleeping with a CPAP respirator for years, so any deterioration in breathing was familiar to us. Living with someone who is suffering but cheerful becomes a way of life, and you carry on. The gritLIT event, where a friend would read my poems, was important to me. Shirl knew this, and said she would be fine by herself for a few hours and I should go.

I got home mid-afternoon to find her in bed. Nothing unusual since she's a night owl. An hour later, she called me, sitting up on the end of the bed. I said, "What's going on?" She replied, "Can't breathe." She wanted to get to a hospital, so I called an ambulance. She never came home again. Twelve days after that she died.

So, the day I left her alone to go to the readings for an hour and receive congratulations, she was quietly losing her battle with the sixty to one hundred new cancers in her lungs. I wasn't there. In his song "Night Drive," Garnet Rogers considers his travels with his brother Stan in the line, "I wish I'd shown you better." I'll always, always feel that.

October 10, Thanksgiving Day: Journal

In the photo, you are lying in a hammock in the garden. You are beautiful. You have eyes of uncompromising kindness, a heart of strength to bear the ills that beset you, an intellect to feed your insatiable curiosity, a will that stopped at nothing short of mastery and more love than I have ever known.

If you were here with me, I would hold nothing back. We would share an honesty we only envied before you died. I should have died first, though going on alone would not have helped you, either.

November 2: Journal

When I gardened, at some point you would always open the window and watch me, and then call out with some sarcastic, funny comment. Today, I pruned and tied the black raspberries, pried the English ivy off the tree trunk, cleaned out the downspouts and gutters, and varnished the birdhouse. No one came to the window. I wasn't gardening for you, or I was but you weren't there.

November 7: Journal

I wore a pair of your new jeans to a poetry reading, and even after having laundered them, I could very faintly detect your cigarette smoke mixing with my body heat. How complex a feeling, to bear on myself the smell of the demon that killed you so young and took you from me. No one else appeared to notice, but I knew.

November 21: Journal

Last night in the gale, I heard noises that I thought were a presence in the house. Grinding noises, louder than the wind blowing down the chimney and opening the fireplace doors. I walked the floors in the dark, looking out all the windows to check for broken branches – nothing. Was it you? You, the one who returns my lost glasses to me, whom I sense standing behind me in my office doorway, who enters my day in any of a hundred different ways? And yet, when I have something to share, when I've done something to show you, you're not there, and I put it away as meaningless or pointless and look for an escape elsewhere, in music or film or food, from the unbearable vacancy of your leaving.

Your absence invades me. I breathe it in, lock it in my lungs. My heart pumps it through my blood, my head aches with it, my stomach and chest heave with it. I walk a crooked line, out of balance. Everything equivocates. I appear to function, to be engaged, to be appreciative. But you know I live with the absence that is everywhere you.

December 5: Journal

Things I Do to Miss You

park on my side of the driveway
sleep on my side of the bed
say "we" and "our house"
shop for more Pearl Bailey (pearl barley)
dry myself with your bath towel
turn down the TV so as not to wake you
leave your voice on the answering machine
leave your office door shut so as not to interrupt you
go in anyway to interrupt you
check my coins for your collectable quarters
wear your Haida key chain as a medallion
wear your two-rings charm on a gold chain
do your 1,000-piece Christmas jigsaw
play your corny Christmas classics
hang your stocking from the mantle
try to donate a kidney to your brother
because you would have if you could have
fill the feeder to attract a cardinal
thank you when one comes

December 12: Journal

I will ask my sons to bury my ashes in a hole below the frost line (I never liked the cold) in Shirl's garden bed. I know the house will be sold and the garden will not likely endure, but whatever fate awaits her remains should await mine also. If this is unsatisfactory to my sons, let the wishes of the living trump those of the dead.

December 31: Journal

On the last day of 2016, I watch three cardinals – one male, two females – feeding in Shirl's garden. In all likelihood, I have seen these same birds and thanked Shirl for their coming many times before. I have thought of them variously as her guardians, her spirit allies, her assurances, her reincarnated soul, and I have felt my cheeks moisten with tears as I watched. I do not anticipate more logical conclusions in the new year that begins tomorrow.

I have accepted an invitation to a New Year's Eve party, a quiet affair with interesting talk among friends and no party favours, whistles, hats or noisemakers. We likely will not make it to midnight. This suits me perfectly. Shirl and I would spend New Year's Eve at home in front of a roaring fire and the TV, watching movies until and often past the time when the ball drops over Times Square. At midnight we'd yell Happy New Year, and then right away, Rabbits! for a month of mutual good luck. We'd kiss the new year in, toast each other with my beer and her Diet Pepsi and, having done our due diligence, go to bed. Tonight, when I get home from the party, I will do the same. Happy New Year, my dear. Rabbits!

A scarlet flash of a northern cardinal settles in the web of lilac twigs. Perhaps he, too, longs for his life-mate, remembering last spring when she perched among the nearby apple blossoms, preening her feathers in readiness. ~

MAN – *Will I be done grieving?*
BIRD – *No, not at all. You are done being hopeless. Grieving is something you're still doing, and something you don't need a [bird] for.*[1]

NOTES

1 Max Porter, *Grief is the Thing with Feathers* (Minneapolis: Graywolf Press, 2015), 103.

CHANGING OUR ADDRESS

Lynn Tait

Personal loss seems to be everywhere these days. Grief is receiving a lot of notice, as if a new emotion had been added to our culture instead of the emotional outpouring of sorrow all of us have experienced since the beginning of time. I buy occasion cards in advance. And I find I run out of sympathy cards before any other Hallmark event. Social media, the Internet, Twitter and the real-timeliness of our lives make grief appear "new" but also show us just how bound together we are. The locations of grief are no longer limited to one's personal headspace and immediate family, rather pain spills out now over vast geographies. We are inundated with books and articles written about grief: dealing with one's own, how to cope with someone else's, what to say or not say and the list goes on. I've written scores of poems about the loss of our only child, Stephen, affectionately called "Steve" or "Stevo," who died in 2012 at the age of twenty-nine from a fentanyl overdose, and I haven't even scratched the surface. As the location of my grief changes, so do the poems. Yet there are places of anguish I still cannot enter, am unable to write about and still refuse to explore. There are bereavement support groups everywhere and for everyone, yet we are still rather awkward about grief, even our own. My son's Facebook page remains intact. His friends and I, cyber and real, send him messages on special dates and when we miss the sound of his voice, his laughter and his fun-loving nature.

Grief seems to be spreading – loss of almost anything seems to be associated with grief. I've seen people devastated over the loss of a pet, which most of us understand. I've heard someone publicly announce they're still reeling over the death of a parent but fail to mention the relationship with their terminally ill family member was almost non-existent, as if grief is a bandwagon to jump on, as if they don't yet fully comprehend the devastation of losing someone, of connections heartbreakingly severed, changing entire lives instantly. And that's just the beginning – with the death of a loved one, this kind of heartache, we are never the same. We live in a different place in our heads and hearts. Our surroundings seem to take on different shapes and colours, creating a dullness that for some of us becomes permanent.

There is much written on what to say to the grief-stricken. Some I agree with, some comments don't bother me in the least but are maddening for others. I don't like to be told how to grieve, especially by people who've had very limited experience with it. Most of my emotions, feelings and thoughts, even years after the initial loss – this grief occurs in my head in all its complexities – are negative: the guilt, the regrets. Our son died during Hurricane Sandy, a landscape-changing occurrence that, overlapping with a life-altering event, also transformed our family's landscape.

I always thought if I did outlive him, he'd lose his life in the service of others, saving someone else. This may sound "romantic," but Steve would jump in before thinking when it came to helping people. This habit was rather annoying as well as nerve-racking. Though I knew this about him, I'm his mother, and I realize we tend to sugar-coat our children's faults and overemphasize certain traits.

His friends still recall his big heart and his humour before anything else. They continue to remember the day of his death and his birthday. Various objects are still left by his gravesite. One of his buddies named his daughter after him.

I believe the location of their grief dwells in guilt. I think they realized they might have received more than they gave. If my husband or I think too deeply within the recesses of our own minds, guilt is the predominate place we go to. Guilt becomes a location, the address being "if only" in the province of regret: If only we had insisted on piano lessons at the age of six. If only we hadn't moved to a different neighbourhood. If only we hadn't worked so much. If only we'd insisted he attend university. If only we had travelled more together as a family. If only we were more aware of his struggles with drugs. Steve was a touchy-feely guy. Held my hand longer than most boys would allow or want. In a poem titled "Grief" I describe the devastation felt when I realized during our private viewing I'd failed to take his hand one last time:

his hands – I did not think of his hands – hold them
one last time –

and the tightening begins in the rib cage,
heart-burrowing worm – the tearing weight – the
   slithering pull –
the slow agony – that mistake – my most painful regret.

It still is.

If only, if only, if only, regret, regret, regret. A message in a constant loop always stamped: return to sender. We all have trouble changing the address and rewriting the message.

My husband and I have tried rewriting our messages, relocating the grief with some surprising success. We have all done this – the sudden resurgence of butterflies or finding coins in strange places seems to be popular, as does the appearance of cardinals, making a habit of paying it forward, whether through charity work or just buying a stranger a coffee. For my husband and I, travelling with and spreading his ashes all over the world helps.

We have placed some of his, and his beloved cat Kilo's, ashes in Sarnia's Lakeview Cemetery, with its trees, gentle slopes and wildlife, people riding bikes, walking or jogging, where, when we drive through the grounds to other parts of town, even if unable to stop, we can see his stone and embedded picture from the road. But we believe Steve is not in just one place; he is everywhere, able to take in and be part of every living thing, and in our travels we DO encounter cardinals in the strangest of places.

Besides the cemetery, his ashes are outside a Florida Crab Shack restaurant, below a hawk's nest, on the field at the Blue Jays' winter stadium and Toronto stadium, too. He's on top of a mountain in Tucson, Arizona; a popular beach in Nassau; Dean's Blue Hole and a tidal pool in Long Island, Bahamas; the Pacific Ocean and the coast of Costa Rica – places teeming with wildlife. Imagine our surprise when, for the first time, we released his ashes in sunlight and calm waters to see him sparkle in a leisurely radiant descent. So fitting! He loved the water, wildlife and snorkelling. He's at a Mediterranean beach in Barcelona; a hill on the edge of a valley in Ronda, Spain; the end of a boat launch in Faro, Portugal; and an Alfama neighbourhood in Lisbon. He's with us on motorcycle tours and always rides shotgun in the car.

Back in Canada, he's on an iceberg and at Cape Spear, Newfoundland. In Sarnia, his cremains have been scattered on the St. Clair River and in nearby Canatara Park, a place with a small lake, nature trails and woodlands, nostalgically referred to as "Tarzanland" by the locals, where we searched for snakes, insects and other animals during his youth.

At home, in our backyard, Nature teaches us the beginning and ending of life every day – the continual struggle to survive. Steve, Kilo and his first cat, June, rest among flowers and rocks, our son, his father and I collected over the years. The Eskimo Sunset maple, planted in Steve's memory, has undergone multiple setbacks and still manages to survive, so far. This tricoloured maple is not a native tree to southwest Ontario and has suffered from lack of water, high winds, storms, severe winters, squirrels breaking off branches and rabbits ripping bark. Still it hangs on, grows taller, but we are always aware each year might well be its last. This young tree teaches us about the completion of cycles, the sudden end to things we hoped would endure or outlast us.

In the house, it's our clock. No amount of common sense will change our minds that after Steve's death, the clock's reluctance to ring out correct gongs at certain times has little to do with mechanics and everything to do with Steve's spirit fooling with it. Our grief – the positive aspect of our emotions, "the missing" – is calmed by this belief, maybe even the faith that Steve, jokester that he was, is still with us. What is even crazier is that my husband started this. Not me. I'm a poet and possess a surreal non-linear idealistic form of silliness, so for me it makes sense that I would have started this idea, not my logical, serious, no-nonsense Virgo man. I am a woman of metaphor, but it was my husband who started saying, "There's Steve," if the clock chimed three times at eleven o'clock. This does not cause a moment of silence or bring tears to our eyes – it's uplifting, humorous and more likely to cause a conversation, a smile – and we feel closer to him. The landscape of our sadness is changed.

We did call a clock repair shop. They'd fix it for a reasonable price. The guts of the clock would have to be replaced. This seemed fine – at first, until the next time the clock rang – one chime instead of three. What happens if we *do* fix the clock? Do we end up losing a part of Steve? Will the house somehow seem emptier, void of fun and games without the mis-ringing of this inanimate object? We even entertained the thought of fixing the clock to see if Steve did in fact control the timepiece. Wouldn't it be amazing and wonderful if even after the clock was "repaired" he still made his presence known, and we could look forward to the occasional non-ringing of twelve bells at midnight or noon! (Steve always did like to shake things up.) Could we take that chance, fix the clock and pray his spirit still plays the "time game" with us? Or leave it as is, and release our grief through the improbability of ghosts and spirits, keeping him in our hearts instead of our heads: that place of cloud and thunder where the time never changes forever locked in a gated community of regret.

The day of the winter solstice 2017, a friend and writing colleague passed away from the same brain cancer as Gord Downie, the Tragically Hip's front man. She was an amazing woman whose grace, quiet nature and patience were as well-known as her gentle poetry. She was loved by all. The clock chimed correctly that entire day. We believe Steve gave us our answer.

WORRY STONES

Jenna Butler

Stones appear magically each year in a field meant to grow something else. They take on all shapes and sizes: small enough to nestle into the hollow of your fist; the shape and heft of a horse's heart; bowed like the wing of a barn swallow in flight. In spite of careful picking, they seem to multiply annually, because somewhere out there, a breeding stone lies under a curl of sod. As long as that motherstone lingers in your field, a crop of offspring will appear each April more bountiful than your wheat. In turning the field, should you find an oddly figured rock, perhaps one sketched with indigo or green like beautiful plumage, it behooves you to take it as far from the field as you can. Drop it into running water to counteract its magic, but keep it beyond the borders of your land, for it is the source of all the problems in the field.

This teaching tale was passed along to me somewhere in my childhood, a distant lesson probably told down generations in a farming community in England where tasks such as picking rocks were annual duties for the youngest in the family. I've heard it in different iterations over the years, between the land I was born on and the land I now call home, but always with the same underhanded current of worry. The story traces a duty of vigilance, whether that duty is as mythic as finding and disposing of a magical stone or simply instructing young ones in the annual task of gathering winter-heaved rocks before the plow finds them. This is a task possessing its own small import on most pieces of arable land – and one not so small for the farmers whose fields start each spring as a crazed pocking of new stones. It is tied to a deep care for the land and a yearly anxiety for its well-being.

Rural communities pocket their griefs like stones curled beneath the surface of the sod. We know who is in a bad relationship but stays, for the stability or for their children, and often both. We know whose friend is more than a little crooked and robbed him blind while he was away for chemo, but we understand that this friend will, once again, be forgiven. There's no way around it: small towns are small towns, and people can only run so far. You forgive or you don't, and you run into that once-friend at the co-op the following week. We know whose wife is on a long, slow rebound from hanta, whose wheat crop was scythed in July by an unexpected hailstorm. Who is giving up and selling out.

We carry each other's griefs like stones, worn with the knowing.

Here is what *I* know.

Muskeg spruce scabbed with gum, and white willow, astringent bark steeped for tea against pain. Bunchberry, Canada violet, ravels of twinflower.

How to read a night of frost ahead in the chill tightening my bare soles on the ground. How to read snow in the cinched halo around a November sun.

That the land will share my grief awhile as I learn to bear its weight.

We clear ground under the tall white spruces closest to our cabin out on the land. There's a natural circle there, a grove of old trees. It feels like a good place, one that channels energy out along the roots, knows how to field it, to let it go.

This is work best done together, not dangerous but intricate, felling the leaning willows with a chainsaw and moving their desiccated limbs to the burn pile. It is work we would do here anyway in time to remove the fire hazard of their branches, but the need for this space gives its creation a certain quiet urgency. My husband understands my impulse to build this garden under the trees, although he does not share the specific grief that drives me here. Striving at this task together is a healthy thing, a clean thing, beneath the high canopy of the spruce, the early autumn light falling in and illuminating the gradually opening ground. When he cuts the chainsaw's engine, we are aware once again of the silence that underpins the forest, the innate calm of this place. The chickadees and nuthatches whiffle down to the feeders on the cabin patio nearby. The brome grass dips its slender heads, heavy with seed. The circle of trees is the right choice.

Grief's internal work is done alone, but there are times in its cycle when we can't see our way clear without another person to shelter our trust. My husband holds space for me: he is present with me in grief, but he doesn't push; he is patient when anger and fear fly out of me in all directions while I learn the slow and necessary navigation through pain. It was his suggestion that we create this memory garden out in the forest, close enough to the cabin that I can visit the grove often, but far enough away that the trees stand in essential solitude. A strong partnership, this. He can see, sometimes, the steps ahead that I might otherwise miss.

On the land, I learn day by day the worry-work of grief, but I know little of memorializing. The garden is created from instinct, opening the space to light and air, to sun through all seasons. On the cleared round of forest floor, we spread a thick layer of willow chip, pale red and damp, smelling of sap and green wood. We set a boundary ring of seven glass lanterns at the clearing's periphery, circling in this space against the eventual dark. At the centre of the garden, we root three perfect birch rounds from the woodpile. At their feet, seven slabs of heartwood, one from each of the big trees we've had to fell over the years as we've built our small farm from the bush. Memory upon memory, circle upon circle, the garden gives itself up to the forest.

The community and the land have taught me that I can carry pain alone for only so long before I need to stop awhile and let it rest, let myself step away, if for no other reason than to meet again the person I am beyond the scope of that loss. The memory garden in its grove of trees acts as that interface, allowing me to part from my grief for a short time when I move beyond its confines.

I imagine each of my daughters as a stone. The eldest, not my own child but the deeply loved daughter of a previous partner, would be twenty-seven this year; I picture her effervescent as quartz, sure and bright, implacable in her young sense of the world. The middle one, forced into my life and body when I was fourteen, would be twenty-two now. I named her after the first fall of snow, but she passed out of the world having never known the winter. I have always seen her, in my mind's eye, as grey – the grey of something that obscures, the drape of prairie mist over the sloughs in September. The curtain drawn on childhood a long time ago, a scumbled gauze. And my third daughter is scarcely more than a pebble, green as the Pacific, barely begun and never known. By the time she came into my life three years ago, my body had paid a lonely debt to silence and pain and fear, and it could no longer carry her.

For many years, I carried the weight of those stones by myself. I buried them deep, not understanding that those weights, those stories of loss and grief, would proliferate beneath the surface. That they would eventually demand to be recognized; that my survival would depend upon that recognition.

The memory garden at our farm was an act of self-preservation. It's only possible to cobble together a life around those hard kernels of grief for so long before the loss riddles everything you do, becomes all that you are. I felt a deep guilt at not having a place to visit my daughters and recognize their presence; as the men who brought them into my world passed beyond it in various ways, I was left alone to carry the weight of my girls' lives and losses. Because there were no bodies, no memorials, I carried that weight constantly, unable to lay it down, unprepared to look away.

In that circle of trees, I can finally let my girls and their stories be. I can set down beside their memorial the weight of their fathers, the cost of their taking. I can be at ease, or as close as I will ever get to ease, with my body and its brokenness. The memory garden is less a growing place than a space of air and light that permits me to find, in the lacunae of world and body, a certain peace. Here, I call my grief by its names and look it in the face awhile.

And the garden allows me to set down that grief after a time and re-enter the world.

I'm not the only woman who holds this grief like a stone in her chest. As I come to learn the depths of the community that surrounds our farm, I know I will encounter others who have lost as I have, and others who have such places to remember, as I have my circle of trees at Larch Grove. But I'm not ready to cast this story beyond the borders just yet. The telling is still new to me, the need. All I can do is trust my daughters' stories, roll them across my tongue. Those stones taste like long years of grief, the sharp bite of salt.

They are teaching me how to speak.

TWO:
THE NEIGHBOURHOOD

MY FRIEND JUNE

Sharon Thesen

June was a connoisseur of qualities, timing, fabrics, child care and home economics. She had wonderful ideas about how to do things that turned out spectacularly well and made everyone happy, including her. She was a talented baker, a magician of the microwave, the stove, the barbecue and the sewing machine. She was pleased with herself and with the results of all her actions. She always had good ideas about what to do with yourself on Boxing Day, and how to entertain houseguests from the coast. She ran daycare centres back in Ontario before she moved to White Rock, BC, and then, fed up with the rain and the traffic, to Kelowna.

June grew up in rural Ontario, in or near what town I don't remember, except that she told me later, when trying to figure out why she got cancer in her mid-fifties, that she thought it may have had to do with exposure to chemicals used in agriculture; and also maybe the stress of having an angry daughter. Her only child, who lived back east, had just had a baby and was finding reasons for June to not visit.

June and I met while walking our dogs in the new subdivision we'd both recently moved to. We had become, in a short time, good friends, the kind of good friends you can be later in life. You know each other in the now; you haven't a long past in common – most of the big changes in your lives happened decades earlier and in other places. Conversations stayed general, there was no point in elaborating details that the other had no context for. Even so, we found lots to talk about, including how strange it was to live in a suburban subdivision, but where else would we have lake views like that and a brand-new house at what was then a very reasonable price?

The subdivision was called South Ridge, and there were about forty houses off a T-shaped roadway. A "park" was made somewhere in the middle and a new road was already being built just above ours. Hundreds of acres of woods, streams and meadows flourished just beyond where the roads ended, having not yet succumbed to the inferno that would engulf the landscape a couple of months later. June and her husband, David, lived a little farther up the hill, while we were closer to cherry orchards and large, old properties that until then had been somewhat out of town. Deer hunters still stalked the woods not far from our houses, back in 2003, when I first met June.

Late one night, after a lengthy heat wave, we were awakened by a thunder clap, and in the morning, a plume of smoke could be seen rising into the sky to the south. This plume, by the time June and I got to the beach that afternoon for our regular swim, was starting to develop an ominous anvil shape on its eastern edge. Two days later, you could hardly see or breathe for the smoke, and there were reports of houses burning in a residential area far to the south, but for some reason we weren't quite sure about that even though evacuation alerts were being handed out in neighbourhoods down the way. We tried to stay calm as falling embers burned holes in our lawn chairs. Paul and I had made a casual arrangement just in case, with friends who lived in Penticton, should worse come to worst, which we didn't think was possible. Surely the fire wouldn't jump the blocks-wide clearing where the big power lines were.

One morning, greatly worried, we decided I'd go down to Penticton while Paul would stay and hold the fort. I drove for two hours through a twilight of smoke and ash to our friends' house. June and David, who had also decided to stay longer, invited Paul for dinner that night. At some point, June went out to the deck and saw the fire coming down the hill. By then, police were going door to door yelling, "Leave now! Leave now!"

Two days later, we didn't even know if our house was still standing. June and David had driven straight back to White Rock the night of the evacuation. It was being said that if you dialed your home number and the line was busy, it meant your house was gone. Paul dialed our number and the line was busy. We were just trying to absorb this when David phoned from White Rock. He, too, had dialed their number and the same thing had happened. Also, he said, June was unable to swallow properly and was in pain and vomiting. I remember what went through my mind then: *our houses have burned down and June is going to die of cancer.*

Our houses hadn't burned down; in fact, there was surprisingly little damage. Three hundred other houses were destroyed, though, and we felt survivor guilt afterwards.

Firefighters had had to abandon our area, but minutes later the wind suddenly changed direction and the fire drove back uphill and went on to consume another neighbourhood, Crawford, to the northeast.

June did die of colon cancer two and a half years later, after refusing surgery and chemotherapy treatments. She would do it her way, which meant alternative modalities. June was not a countercultural person. She had a genteel and steely Ontario vibe about her, which made her decision seem incongruous, but she persisted even though she was frightened. June had an excess of what psychologists call "executive function." She flew back to Ontario to see her daughter and her daughter's two children, and her daughter visited later when June was making plans to admit herself to hospice, just for a while. We would lie on her bed together when I visited; she was too tired to sit up.

After some serious pleading from her doctor, June agreed to try *one* chemotherapy treatment. But she would not put up with her hair falling out all over the place. She cried, I cried, the hairdresser cried as her hair – beginning to grey now – spiralled from the blade of the shaver. The treatment was a disaster. No more, said June. German New Medicine was now her alternative. She would lie on amethyst mats to increase her internal body temperature, and it worked, in that she lived a year longer than the six months she was allotted at the time of her diagnosis. During that year, she gardened, made quilts, slept and endured her symptoms. I have never known such a brave person, except for someone else I knew who did take the full roster of chemotherapy, surgery, radiation and years of Tamoxifen afterwards.

When June died, Paul and I were in Hawaii on holiday. A voice mail when we got back said she'd died of a stroke after spending a "lovely" – that would have been her word – afternoon with David at the hospice. It was around Christmastime. My friend Maria once said, every death is different. You never know whose death will cause you the most grief.

The blackened-stick remnants of the forest soon gave way to hundreds of new houses, McMansions chockablock down row after row of new streets where creeks and coyote dens and deer meadows used to be. We moved away a year after the fire, a few months before June was diagnosed with colon cancer. I remember her helping me pack boxes and my sensing that we shouldn't be moving just then. *Forgive me, June*, I say to her now. I should have insisted she follow the doctor's orders; I shouldn't have been supportive of her decision to go her own way, which I knew she agonized about privately. I might have been able to change her mind. She might still be alive. That thought is the one that hurts the most; and yet at the time, when June was suffering, there was something so serenely valiant about her that her choice of action seemed unassailable.

I asked June at some point if she was keeping notes about her various alternative and complementary treatments and medications, and she said she was. I'd like to see those notes sometime – or maybe I wouldn't, but they should be published somewhere, for general edification. For the story of a life lost to well-meaning incompetencies of every type and kind. A life lost to error, miscalculation, denial and hubris, aided and abetted by the protocols and wish-granting of a friendship far too brief.

COQUITLAM HOUSE

Onjana Yawnghwe

This is the story of a house. It sits near the end of a cul-de-sac, atop a steep hill of a driveway. The exterior was once beige and brown, but has since been painted white with a dark green trim. Two levels: windows on the left, and a balcony and garage on the right. Shutters once bookended the windows, but have since been removed after they started falling apart, one by one.

The house is filled with decades-old knick-knacks: tiny silver seal figurines, a German music box, a plastic shoe key chain, one-inch models of army tanks. On the top shelf of a cabinet is a Buddhist altar, cluttered with small metal Buddha statues from Thailand and Burma, passed on from generation to generation. Portraits of the family populate some of the walls: a smiling brother and sister, a stern-looking man in ceremonial garb, a dinner party, smiling Asian faces turned toward the camera. Other walls hold large oil paintings: a blonde woman in red reclining on a sofa, or a Shan palace, a portrait of a young couple in the 1960s, wearing shades.

*

The master bedroom is where it happens, at the end of a long and strange road: the medical appointments, the hospital admission, the biopsy, CT scans, the MRIs, the three-month stay in Royal Columbian Hospital, the uncertain prognosis, the initial denial of palliative care and eventual palliative care at home. This is the room where my father dies, aged sixty-five, just days after he comes home from the hospital.

They have trouble bringing up the hospital bed and stretcher, climbing the steep driveway and stairs. My mother had folded up the futon bed into a sofa and pushed it against the sliding glass door to make room. The plastic bed with my father's emaciated body is the centre of the world. After he arrives home he sleeps most of the time, with brief bouts of wakefulness. "*Por*, can you hear me?" "*Por*, are you in pain?" The silent dark eyes searching but glancing blankly. Sometimes a nod, then a closing of the eyes. Sometimes a "yes" or "no," but nothing more. The doctors and nurses assure us he isn't in pain – no cringing, crying, no apparent discomfort, what they call non-verbal signs of pain. The nurse gives us a bottle of morphine, intending to later insert a line into the body for the medication, but they never get around to it. *Is he in pain?* We wonder and wonder.

It is summer, but I barely remember the heat. In the house, friends, aunts and uncles we've known for years. We take turns going in and out of the room, sitting beside him, doing nothing but listening to his breathing, waiting for him to wake up. The sounds of the small TV on in the background.

Days later, his breathing changes, his intake becomes shallower and pauses between prolonged breaths. He barely wakes up anymore. He stops eating and drinking. We know the end is near. My mother says, "We need to give him permission to die," and we are alone with him; we tell him we love him, that it's okay to go, that we will be okay here, that my brother's on a plane on his way here but he knows that you love him, it's okay to go, be at peace, don't worry about us.

And that day we listen to him breathe, his breaths becoming fainter and quicker and sometimes a gasp, and finally they stop. I don't know whether it's night or day, or how many hours have passed. Perhaps a Buddhist prayer is said, there are so many things I don't remember. The doctor comes to call the death, and she offers us sleeping medications. "Many people," she says, "have trouble sleeping during difficult times like these." We decline. I remind her to take the unopened bottle of liquid morphine with her. The funeral home picks up the body.

The next time I see my father he is in the casket at the funeral home in Burquitlam. He is cold, his skin is strangely waxy and yellow, and he does not look like himself. His face is stretched and smoothed in a strange way, lips pulled too tightly. I'm reminded of how my grandmother looked after she died two years earlier, how the skin becomes dusky, leathery, dry and taut.

Before Coquitlam, we lived in an apartment in Mount Pleasant. One day our parents came home from visiting my aunt and uncle in Coquitlam and suddenly declared, "We bought a house!" They had been driving and saw an "open house" sign, and somehow the price was right and they fell in love with it. My brother and I met the news with dismay. We liked living in East Vancouver, we knew all the buses and how to get around; we weren't intimidated by dark streets or traffic or raised voices. But this Coquitlam house was in the middle of nowhere, built on the slope of a mountain so there were hills everywhere. The carpets were old, shaggy and yellow. The wallpaper was ugly. I didn't know what to do with a yard. When we moved, my twenty-year-old brother took this as his opportunity to move out.

My parents loved the house. To them, it was their happy ending, the proof that coming to Canada from Burma (after a few years in Thailand) was all worth it, that we as a family had "made it." All those years of struggling – of never going on vacation or to restaurants, of working all the time – had paid off. Over the years, they made minor improvements: hardwood floors for the living area, new carpets for the bedrooms, new tile for the entryway, retiling the downstairs bathroom. Painting accent walls: pastel yellow and blue. But the 1970s wallpaper remained. My mother said that the hills of Coquitlam always reminded her of Shan State in Burma; she was used to mountain air. From the kitchen window you could glimpse a sliver of the Fraser River, glistening in the daylight.

When we moved to Coquitlam, the world shrank; there was house and walking and school then back again. There was grass everywhere instead of concrete, and people drove lazily on deserted streets. You had to walk slowly – the slowness seeped into you somehow and you could smell the grass, the magnolia trees, the rain rolling down those steep hills.

My father worked as a political consultant for an NGO with the goal of Burmese democracy, and travelled often to and from Thailand. After a trip in March, he complained of more and more tiredness but resisted seeing a doctor, getting a haunted, empty look in his eyes. We noticed he began to have trouble walking, leaning a little on one side, and became quieter, more subdued. His bouts of anger came less frequently, and his opinions about news and politics dimmed and dampened.

After dinner, it was his daily habit to go downstairs to his office to write political papers and do research. One night I came by to say good night when I noticed he seemed to be concentrating very hard on what he was typing. I looked at the monitor and was shaken. On the screen "jjjjjjjkkkkkkkkkkkjjjj;;;;;" was typed by his slow and deliberate fingers. The world turned dark. He was a man who loved reading, who wrote every day, who had one of the sharpest minds, and now here he was, language inexplicably lost.

One day we were watching TV and a commercial came on, a clever one meant to be funny, and my father suddenly asked, "What happened?" It took a beat for me to get it. He was asking me to explain how the commercial worked. He had never asked me to explain anything before, not one thing, because he always knew everything. He was the smartest of us.

Weeks passed and he retreated into silence, sometimes blankly looking into space, answering with only a few words. A perplexed gaze. Bizarre behaviour, like spooning his birthday gift of brandy over rice or trying to pee in a little wastepaper basket in the living room. Sleeping most of the day and night. No longer able to drive or undertake basic functions on his own. Gait increasingly unsteady. But sometimes his old self came back. Once as I was downstairs getting ready to leave for a class, he suddenly looked down from the banister and asked, "Do you want me to send you?" like he'd done so many times when I went to school. I was caught by surprise by the kindness of this familiar act and blinked away tears, calling out brightly, "No, it's okay, Daddy, I can take the bus." "Are you sure?" "Yes. Thanks, though." The manifestations of his illness and rapid decline became sudden, repeated shocks; who my father had been was quickly crumbling. He looked but could not name, lost in his own home, through the warren and cul-de-sac of his own mind.

Finally: hospitalization. Diagnosis of an inoperable diffuse tumour of the brain. A mass in the brain stem. Swallowing difficulty. Sepsis from an infected IV site. Adult briefs around his emaciated hips. Bedsores. We visited every day, brought food from home. Sometimes he recognized us, other times his barely audible voice asked, "Who are you?" We, too, were lost, not knowing what was going on, and no one seemed to explain anything to us. Or perhaps they did explain but we were too shell-shocked to understand. It is ironic and cruel that a man who loved the spoken and written word so, a man who prized intelligence above all qualities, so quickly lost any ability to communicate or reason. My uncle said the person we knew, the dad I loved, was no longer there. But I was skeptical. *He's not there? But where is he?*

I often dream about the house, and find my father there. He is mostly silent, a presence, someone in the background. But he is well and smiling. Our family is together again, even with my brother. The yellowness of my bedroom walls, how

I loved those walls that I painted, even though everyone said the colour was garish and tacky. The sickly flowery smell of blooming lilacs, which always made me think of Whitman's "When Lilacs Last in the Dooryard Bloom'd." A gentle calico cat on the windowsill. Stillness, silence.

I've been trying to convince my mother to sell the house and move to a smaller place, nearer to transportation and stores. It has been sixteen years since my dad died, and many of his things are still stored in closets. His books are still on the bookshelves. The souvenirs he'd brought from his travels – like a Eugene, Oregon, magnet; a miniature music box; figures of German children dancing – are still displayed in the house.

My mother continues to be in good health, but her arthritis is getting worse and she's having more and more difficulty walking. Though she is sharp and social and busy all the time, I encourage her to think about the future. Think about that hill, the driveway, those stairs. She refuses for the most part. She says, "I think I'm going to be okay for the next three or four years." But I worry and worry.

A parent's death is a common occurrence, and this story is hardly an exceptional one. But when I think of a person and all he or she contains, all that is lost within that person, all that is left are memories residing in another person's brain, whatever distorted version those memories may take. The objects contained inside a house, how we still see a hospital bed in a room even though it's long gone, how pictures that are taken down leave the faint traces of their borders. What will this house be when it is emptied and sold? Will it still appear in my dreams, the yellow room, the strange glitter on the popcorn ceiling that looks like distant stars? The temptation to hang on to everything he touched.

One is tempted to think: the air must have changed here, the walls must have retained an essence of that brief life. The steps of my father, from Rangoon (Yangon), to the jungles of Burma, to Chiang Mai, to Mount Pleasant and to Coquitlam – where have they led to? This house is where he found himself, where he chose to be at the end of his life.

The house has always been quiet, suffused with a peacefulness. It is a place where you feel like nothing bad can happen; the rooms cocoon you into a kind of safety. I hope my father felt that before he died, that he felt safe and loved. It's hard to know what goes on inside a person, what goes on inside death. I hope he thought of home, wherever that was for him, whether Coquitlam or Shan State or some other place, perhaps inside a book he'd read in childhood. I hope he sensed somehow that he was here, in this house.

LANDING

Katherine Bitney

Odd sort of grief, this, for a child I never knew, who was born with half a skull and died within a few days of birth. She could not have lived, anyway, not without a proper head. It was 1960 and I was thirteen. She came and went so swiftly she could have been on the wing. We named her Halina, and she was buried in a small white coffin in what remains an unmarked grave in Woodlawn Cemetery, in Saskatoon. A little sister who wasn't, who couldn't be.

How does this become a grief then, an old grief I am still writing about nearly six decades past the coming and going of this little unmet sister? Perhaps precisely that – because she slipped past us, slipped away after the long promise of her coming.

Yes. I was thirteen, and it was June. My aunt was readying for her wedding, my grandparents were coming in from England. And my mother brought a long-awaited child to term.

It was immediately clear that the infant would not be able to live: she was born with a half-formed skull, without a proper brain. But at thirteen, what did I know, what did I understand? From the moment she was born, and even though I knew she was not expected to live, nevertheless I hoped, bargained with the divine, raged, paced up and down the back garden, up and down, begging, until, within a few days of her birth, she died.

My mother was still in hospital when we buried Halina. A priest, a tiny white coffin, a few prayers, a sprinkle of holy water. Small open grave. I did not understand what exactly had happened, and my mother was vague about how this death came to be. But I understand this much now, that this type of sorrow has always come to families, still does. There are always starts to life that don't, can't succeed, where the spirit turns back for one reason or another; the body will not do, is incomplete, too weak, won't function for a proper life. So it was with Halina.

We lived not far from the cemetery, just down the back road from our home, where 36th Street meets the railway then crosses 1st and 2nd Avenues. Maybe fifteen minutes if you stroll. Both my parents are now buried there.

Woodlawn is an old-fashioned cemetery, or at least it was, the original sections ringed and watched over by big silent elms, the enormous sky of the prairie. Little concrete huts, family crypts dot the lawns. Walking paths wind among gravestones, markers, trees, among clumped plantings of lilacs, peonies you know are old, planted when the cemetery first opened. It is one of those cemeteries whose dead are everywhere, not just their bodies, bones, but their presence – it's palpable, altering the air, filling it. Their peace, their knowing embrace envelops you when you walk it. As though when you pass through the iron entry gates you are finally putting your feet on the path home. The dead want you with them, it seems, they welcome you, and a piece of you becomes your dead self, taken up into the air, gathered into their circles of watchers, greeters, those still held to the earth in this place that is and is not the living world. In the branches of the upper world, the tree canopy, gabby crows hold power, hold that world in place with their bird feet, peer down at you as you pass. Jackrabbits rule the underworld, hide in the thickets of caragana and lilac, bound across the lawns, summer and winter, grass and snow. Here we left Halina in her little coffin to walk with the dead or fly off to another portal, into this world again, or another.

A couple of years before she herself died, my mother expressed a desire to find the child's grave. This, much to my surprise; in all the years since Halina died, my mother had never been to the grave, nor had she sought it, did not know where in the cemetery it was. But now she wanted to perform a small ceremony to the child's memory; find some peace for herself for this deep, old loss, the incomplete parting, and put down the stone of it, as she herself might have said. My mother had spoken even of wanting to put up a stone there, a proper gravestone with name and dates on it, but never did in the end.

On a warm day in early summer we walked together up the back alley to the cemetery office and asked for directions to the plot, for the number on the cement post that marked the little grave. We found the grave right where I remembered standing when I was thirteen, on a slight slope in what was, in 1960, a newly opened section of the cemetery. Now, in the 1990s, when we went to find the grave, it was circled by tall trees and well-established shrubs that I recalled being just saplings back then, freshly planted. The grounds were covered now by a thick lawn where I remembered only new grass and open dirt when we buried Halina.

My mother and I scraped away the leaves and lawn from the small cement post, and verified the number. Then my mother backed away and stood a little apart, said, You do it. Push come to shove, she could not. So I set about the small ceremony she had decided upon: smudged the grave with sage, and spoke to the spirit, calling her by name. If she came, hovered near, then she surely heard me utter the name of the child she did not choose to become. I called her nonetheless to let her know she was not forgotten. That her mother and sister were here to do her honour, say we remembered her. I pushed a crystal, a small amethyst (my mother was fond of amethyst), into the earth near the head of the grave. Laid down a bouquet of early garden flowers. Had she lived, Halina would have been in her forties.

And for that short time, in that little ceremony, I carried my mother's grief as well as my own, brought my mother's old sorrow to her lost daughter. Two griefs, you might say, and now that my mother is gone, only mine left. And I could not tell you what my own grief was, or is, or if it ever conformed to what one imagines grief to be – a deep, intense suffering of the spirit, weeping, a hole, a weight in the heart, on fire with pain, unfathomable longing. Rather, it seems as if a ghost I have carried all these years tucked in a pocket of my spirit, or a cleft or marking scratched on the mind's walls, something – or things – huge, indecipherable, unnameable that got rolled into the tumble of years that followed, the birth of two brothers soon after Halina's passing. Life moves on, always, not stopping for our small sorrows.

And I don't feel the sorrow of this one, not anymore. Not as I did when I was thirteen. Grief has turned itself into acknowledgement of the heft of this coming and going in its time. And I remind myself, too, that we were all, at that time, immigrants, born elsewhere. This little life, Halina, was the first of our family born in Canada, and the first of us to put her body back to its earth, her tiny bones a marker that we were now indeed rooted here, that we were at last tangled in the land.

EVERYTHING TURNS AWAY

Steven Heighton

About suffering they were never wrong,
The Old Masters: how well they understood
Its human position: how it takes place
While someone else is eating or opening a window
or just dully walking along.

– W.H. Auden, *Musée des Beaux Arts*

1.

The first of June, 2015, was also the first day of ideal summery weather – hot but not humid, the grass and young leaves as freshly green as they would get, the verges of lilac along the old railway line in exuberant bloom. We were driving west into the franchise fringes of town in a silver Toyota Corolla that had rolled off the assembly line near the end of the previous century. We meant to test drive several less-used Toyotas at a dealership overlooking a postcard marina on a Lake Ontario bay.

A salesman named Walter – heavy, bespectacled, delivering his pitches in the laconic monotone of a man who has learned not to get his hopes up – introduced us to the three prospects I'd found online. One was a new-looking black Prius Hybrid that cost about $5,000 more than we were ready to pay. I'd thought I might be able to bargain, but Walter, in his anaesthetized drawl, apologized that in this case the price was final. Still, the crimson Camry was promising – the paint looked fresh, the odometer reading was modest and the price was within our range. Walter handed me the key, slapped a magnetic test-drive license plate into the slot above the rear fender and off we drove. He sat beside me, raking his hand through an auburn comb-over that the wind kept compromising, while my wife, Mary, and seventeen-year-old daughter, Elena, sat in the back.

"Lovely day for a drive, isn't it, Steve?" drawled Walter. In some retail circles, I guess, they still believe in punctuating every sentence with the target customer's name – a gambit that seems touchingly antiquated. Aren't we all too savvy nowadays for such obvious sales cons? But we're also lonelier and needier, so maybe charades of kindness and kinship still trigger a gratified response after all.

We, I write, as if there's a parity of loneliness between mere melancholics, like myself, and the catastrophically depressed. I've wondered if I have the right to frame this story – by which I mean, translate and shape such harrowing data. Walter went on personalizing his sales script with *Steve*s as he directed me along what he called "test-drive route numero uno." The route comprised urban and rural stretches, and a drag strip of vacant highway where you could assess a car's acceleration. The Camry had a lot more pickup than our failing Corolla.

We were returning to the dealership the same way we'd set out, on a busy four-lane road that ran alongside the backyards of modest suburban houses from the '60s or '70s, their decks or patios visible some thirty metres away through the trees. It was along this stretch that I became aware, despite Walter's autopilot patter, that behind us Mary and Elena were anxiously discussing something.

Mary tapped me on the shoulder.

"Excuse me" – this more to Walter, who was talking – "I think we should pull over for a second."

I asked what was going on.

"We need to back up. Elena thinks something's wrong back there."

"With the car?" Walter asked with a resigned sigh.

"She thinks someone might be hurt."

I pulled over onto the gravel shoulder and stopped. Elena leaned forward as I turned to look back, her face serious, close to mine. She said, "I saw something the first time we went by, but that was from the far lane. I just saw again, closer. I think a guy is hurt, maybe unconscious."

I started to back up along the shoulder. Mary said, "She had to point him out to me. Maybe he was drunk and fell. He's lying on his deck. She says he hasn't moved since the first time we passed."

"I think he might be bleeding," Elena said.

"She thought he might be wearing a red cap."

"He's there, Dad!"

I stopped again. For the first time on our test drive, silence from Walter.

"His face is still upside down," Elena said. "His head's back over the edge."

"Probably sleeping one off," Walter said. "I can't see anything, but then I'm due for new specs."

"It's not a red cap," Elena said quietly.

I looked hard but couldn't see the man, though I saw the deck, the patio doors, a white brick bungalow. From my point of view, the branch of a large tree beside the road was hiding part of the deck.

"Could be drugs, too," Walter said. "He'll probably be okay, though."

"He's not okay," Elena said.

I pulled back onto the road, U-turned, accelerated up the inner lane and veered left on a yellow light just as it turned red. Silence in the car – Walter rigid, arms stretched straight in front of him, thick vein-less hands bracing the dashboard. I drove a block west and turned south onto a quiet residential street.

"Here?"

"I think so," Elena said.

I pulled in at the curb in front of a landscaped front yard: groomed flower beds, hedges, a blue spruce symmetrical as an artificial Christmas tree. Beyond it, a white bungalow. Picture window, drapes drawn. The vacant driveway recently paved. As I jumped out, Mary said, "Don't go behind the house yet – knock on the door."

"Why?"

"Could be a drug thing – there might be someone back there."

Walter was staring ahead through the windshield with unblinking eyes.

"Be careful, Dad!"

Elena's concern was touching and then disturbing as it hit me that she, with her sharp vision, had seen something we couldn't, something "not okay." I walked toward the house, my legs weightless with adrenaline. As always in situations of potential emergency, I was excited; also worried about the fallen man; also anxious about seeming a busybody, puncturing a stranger's privacy, maybe antagonizing some hostile type whose friend or customer had passed out on the back deck.

I rapped on the solid door. From the other side, a detonation of high-pitched barking. The outburst subsided until I knocked again. I looked back at the car. Mary and Elena – faces side by side – watched me through the open back window. Walter, too, had now turned his pale, despairing face in my direction. I walked past the garage, rounded the corner and ran along the concrete walk that led to the backyard.

I emerged into the yard and froze. Ten feet away, a man was lying face up on the sunlit pine of the deck, his head lolling back over the edge as if craning to look across the yard to the road. Because the deck was the height of my chest, he lay directly in front of me. A grey-green face under streaks and spatters of dried blood. The eyes shut hard. On his emaciated torso, as if placed there lengthwise, a polished mahogany cane. Cane, emaciated, old or ailing – he has slipped, fallen, smacked his head. Unconscious? No, it's too late. He's gone. I have never seen a body look so utterly vacated.

These impressions occupy maybe two or three seconds. I'm caught inside a coroner's forensic snapshot. No: it's not a finished image but a fresh print, still developing, the polished cane transforming into the stock of a rifle – no, something shorter, thicker, a shotgun fallen onto the man's torso. Barrel toward the face. The blood there not from facial wounds but splattered up from below. I can't see the wound, or somehow don't see it, in fact I'm already turning and fleeing back toward the car. The passengers gape as I run toward them. I leap in, slam the door, start the car and babble words at them: old man, shotgun, suicide, dead.

One reason to explore a horrific event in non-fictional instead of fictional terms is that some of its key details might seem implausible in a short story. It is 2015. In a speeding vehicle sit three middle-aged adults, one of them a used car salesman. A teenager is with them. And not one of these four individuals is carrying a phone. My daughter has left hers in our car in the parking lot at the dealership. Walter has always seen these drives as a chance to get away from calls, he explains – adding softly, hopelessly, as if assuming I'll ignore him, "Better not speed, Steve . . . We're almost there . . . If he passed a while ago, a minute won't matter."

Silence from the back seat. I look in the rear-view mirror: Elena staring fixedly out her window. We reach the dealership a few minutes later. Mary and Elena decide to wait outside in the parking lot while Walter leads me in through the showroom to his open-concept cubicle. It's like the mock-up of an office on a stage: three walls that go partway to the ceiling, no front wall at all. He gestures toward his chair, his desk, an office phone. I sit and key in 911. I try to speak calmly, quickly. A burning current crawls beneath my scalp. The pulse in my jaw is like a second heartbeat. The dispatcher, as if new to the job or too sensitive for it, sounds genuinely shaken.

"I wonder if I should have stayed with him," I say, feeling queasier as it hits me: by leaving the scene I might have done something unconscionable. The body is alone, as it must have been for who knows how long before we arrived, and this condition – of almost interstellar solitude – is a terrible insult and indignity.

"No," the dispatcher says. "There was a gun there, you had to leave."

She gets me to repeat the address, sends two police cars and an ambulance, then keeps me on the line to collect my details – address, telephone number – as well as Walter's. He's leaning against the back hatch of a gleaming charcoal-grey SUV, polishing the lenses of his glasses with a Kleenex as I recite coordinates into the phone.

I hang up and stare at my hand, still gripping the receiver. The hand looks prosthetic. My wristwatch says 12:16. I half-see Walter approaching his desk, approaching me, this stranger in his chair. He leans down and – as if gently reminding me of the masculine duty to push on with life's errands in the face of disaster – murmurs, "Dare I ask, Steve, if you've made a decision about the Camry?"

Two hours later, a cop parked his motorcycle in front of our house. I led him around to the side porch and we sat down. He drank strong-smelling coffee out of a stainless steel mug, while I tried to sip a beer that I wanted to guzzle. I wanted something stiffer than beer but wondered if I was already violating some statute by drinking while providing a sworn statement. The man was messily printing my account on foolscap with a pencil. I tried to describe exactly what I'd seen and done – often a challenge for a fiction writer, although not in this case. The incident seemed – still seems – to deny any license to the part of me that compulsively reshapes or redacts experiences.

The cop was tall, had an action-figure physique, and wore aviator shades and motorcycle boots. Despite the glare, he removed his sunglasses, exposing thoughtful blue eyes and long lashes.

"Such a beautiful day, too," I said moronically.

"Those tend to be the worst ones," he said. "It's a myth that Christmas is the worst time."

Still buzzing, hardly able to sit still, I blurted that maybe the first true summer day feels like a leering "fuck you" to someone whose inner world is gripped in winter. The cop inclined his head. After a moment, he said he hadn't gone into the backyard with the paramedics – he didn't need to see that sort of thing, he'd seen one too many.

I asked about the dead man and, a little to my surprise, the cop related as much as he knew – not much, but enough to collapse my assumptions and deductions. The victim was not old, in just his late fifties. He didn't live alone, although on the morning of his death he was alone, except for that dog I'd heard barking.

"We're trying to track down his wife. Looks like she went out of town for the weekend."

"So he planned this – waited for her to leave," I said, instantly replacing my old assumptions with new ones. *She was with another man and didn't realize he knew. Or, there was no other man, but she was leaving him anyway.*

"And he recently retired from the military," the cop said.

"Could he have been over in Afghanistan?" I asked. Then added, "No. Probably too old."

Was I making the cop uneasy? Likely he was unused to such persistent curiosity and reflexive deduction – the professional habits of fiction writers and investigative journalists, along with private detectives, gossips and conspiracy theorists.

I told the cop how surprised I was that no one had seen or heard a thing. He explained that one neighbour did hear something, around 10:00 a.m., but figured it was a big firecracker.

"So he was lying there for two hours."

"I'm afraid so."

The cop gave me contact details for mental health professionals that we, and especially Elena, might want to consult. As he got to his feet, he said, "You should be proud of your daughter. Good eyes." He pointed to his own eyes as he slid his sunglasses back on. "And she chose to speak up."

The realization that your child is further evolved than you were at her age both humbles you and makes you proud – that she's conscientious, empathetic, an adult in a world understaffed by adults. All that. But she will have to carry something heavier than you ever did at seventeen, something that might linger for years on the threshold of her sleeps.

2.

For ten mornings afterward I checked the obituaries on the website of the local newspaper until I found it. I didn't recognize the face in the overexposed black and white photo; it looked much fuller and younger than the blood-streaked face I'd glimpsed. But other details made me all but certain: the date of death, the code phrase "died suddenly," and a reference to retirement from a logistical job in the military.

An online check to link the surname to the house address came up positive: a paving company listed his driveway as a recent contract.

I made a note of the memorial service date.

From the beginning, I'd felt that if there was a service, and if I found the information in time, I should try to attend. Again forming an assumption out of skimpy evidence and ready stereotypes, I'd decided that few mourners would be present. A final existential insult. The military, I guessed, might dispatch some kind of small delegation, but who could say? Elena told me she thought she might want to attend as well. Our intention was to enter quietly, sit at the back and slip out before any next of kin could approach and ask about our connection with the deceased.

On the morning of the memorial service, she decided not to go. I didn't ask her to explain her decision. I put on some decent clothes but then, agonizing, changed back into my summer writing gear – cargo shorts and a T-shirt – before deciding last minute that I had to go after all. I dressed again and ran out the front door, re-knotting my tie as I jogged the five blocks to the funeral home chapel.

Sitting at the back turned out to be the only option. At least two hundred people, dozens of them in military dress uniform, packed the room. There were children, and there were teenagers, too, who looked genuinely distraught, not simply dragooned into the pews. My sense of relief was twofold: people had come to mourn the man after all and, for that very reason, I could come and go anonymously.

The widow, barely able to walk, was helped up the aisle by bulky men who looked awkward in ill-fitting suits and loose-knotted ties. Over the next hour she remained seated and sobbing at the front, while others got up to speak at the lectern. Then a priest with a bald head, a boyish face and an irrepressibly sunny demeanour read a eulogy the widow had written. The content and tone made it clear that the manner of the man's death was no secret. In his late forties he had slid into depression and then, developing ailments unspecified in the eulogy, had to give up or cut back on the physical outlets that had helped him cope: beer-league baseball, fly-fishing and, more recently and devotedly, gardening. It came back to me: the landscaped front yard, the trimmed hedges, the parterred and graded flower beds that – come to think of it – had been sparsely flowered despite the season. Maybe just perennials, the stubborn aftermath of his endeavour.

In the room where I write, I un-shelve a plump, important-looking anthology and turn to the poem "Musée des Beaux-Arts," in which W.H. Auden reflects on Pieter Bruegel the Elder's painting *Landscape with the Fall of Icarus:*

> How everything turns away
> Quite leisurely from the disaster; the plowman may
> Have heard the splash, the forsaken cry,
> But for him it was not an important failure; the sun shone
> As it had to on the white legs disappearing into the green
> Water.

In a footnote, the anthologists observe that the figures in Bruegel's composition have not only failed to notice Icarus plunging out of the sky but also "a dead body in the woods." I quickly find a reproduction of the painting online. Locating the overlooked body is less easy, but eventually – using the magnifying tool to search the woods beyond a field that a farmer and his horse are ploughing – I spot him. Only his face shows clearly, inverted, staring upward, white against the dark forest floor. I recoil from the screen; his positioning and pallor strongly recall the face of the man on the deck.

Could Auden have missed the figure? He wrote his poem after examining the painting in the Musées royaux des Beaux-Arts in Brussels and must have studied the work closely. I assume he saw but chose to ignore that secondary, nameless casualty and to focus on Icarus. If so, it was the right decision. Adding a stanza of reflections on the dead stranger would have herniated the poem, introducing a distracting sidebar, like dropping a second protagonist into a short story.

But visual art works differently, and the face in the woods is integral to the painting. On one level, it serves as a memento mori, one of those small skulls that Renaissance artists planted in the margins of their works as quiet reminders of mortality. And because of its placement on the left side of the canvas, the head also serves as a compositional balance to Icarus, who is plunging into the sea on the lower right side. The balancing works anatomically as well: the dead man's face, along with a bit of his dark-clad torso blending into the undergrowth, physically completes Icarus, of whom we see only a pair of white legs.

Each one's unwitnessed fate echoes the other's, yet the hidden victim seems so much more forlorn. Icarus, after all, is the namesake of the painting, the title of which will direct any viewer to search out and find his submerging form. Nor is Icarus hard to find: his legs, in contrast to the gloomily shaded face in the woods, are lit by the setting sun. Above all, Icarus is an illustrious figure – a sort of misbehaving celebrity, a universal metaphor, a byword to the point of cliché.

*

At the chapel, the jaunty priest, still failing to funeralize his demeanour, read from Psalm 34: *The Lord is close to the brokenhearted. He rescues those whose spirits are crushed.*

A sense of being unseen, alone and spectral, must be a root sorrow for many of the broken; yet there's more than one way of not being seen. You can feel insignificant to the point of invisibility or – while living an outwardly successful, hence *visible,* life – sink under the weight of a pain unapparent to the world.

Maybe Icarus, that golden boy, was a suicide too.

As for those who feel invisible, suicide may simply finalize a self-perceived erasure. Maybe these few thousand words are all trying to say the same thing: you were seen, hence a little less alone, during the two hours after your death.

At home I studied the program from the service. The photo on the front showed a man in his late twenties or early thirties, lanky, fit in the implicit manner of people who work physically but don't frequent weight rooms. His stance: confident but not cocky. Relaxed grin. He's wearing a white T-shirt half tucked into faded jeans and, improbably, a red baseball cap, like the one Elena first thought he might have on. Behind him, a chain-link backstop and beyond that a baseball diamond. Judging by the light and the state of the outfield grass, it's late spring.

I'd set him in motion on that ripening field, loping and tossing the ball to friends, fielding grounders with that easygoing grin or wincing into the sun as he tracks a pop fly. Later, we return to the bleachers and gather around a Styrofoam cooler packed with squat, iodine-brown bottles of Brador that he and his friends snap open with their lighters.

Little older than my daughter is now, I barely say a word, shyly thrilled to be present, swigging beer, humoured by men who are firmly at home in their adult lives.

Trying to finish this piece – trying to pin down, after my various misconstructions, whatever was solidly knowable – I decided to compare my recall of his home and neighbourhood to the reality. But I couldn't drive out there; our Corolla was back in the shop. So I turned to Google Street View.

In that eerily paused, preserved little world, the sun was high, the trees in bud but not yet in leaf – that equivocal pre-season in Kingston when the light, unfiltered by greenery, is dazzling, yet the winds off the lake remain wintry. I clicked on a link and found a date for the images: mid-April, just over a year before the suicide.

I began on the main road from which Elena first glimpsed him, but I couldn't tell which backyard was his. I navigated round to his own street. Again, nothing looked right. I checked my notes for his address, then left-clicked back up the street in blurring little surges.

Finally I recognized the house. The blue spruce looked more familiar by the moment, as did the fieldstone half-fence that I only now recalled, and those terraced garden beds raked and ready for spring flowers. In the foreground at the bottom of the driveway sat a phalanx of brown paper yard-waste bags, evenly packed to the top, and behind them a bundle of neatly tied deadfall and trimmed branches. I glided ghostlike back down the street: no one else had left anything out for collection. Did the neighbours not bother with their yards or had the man always tidied up and set out his refuse early in the season, ahead of collection day?

Gardening is a promissory, optimistic act. To sow is to project, to cast your faith forward into the next season or the following spring. Stumbling on this evidence of his diligence and care – this generative intention still active just a few hundred days before he blew out his heart – moved me very much.

Now I imagine the Street View vehicle, with its mounted camera, passing along the main road not when it did but some thirteen months later, the beautiful morning of his death. If I and Walter, among hundreds or thousands of others, missed his face amid the branches and shadows of his backyard, then the Street View curators who screen the panoramas for legal reasons might have missed him, too. Certainly they would have missed him. The image would still be saved online, his face half hidden in the landscape.

DISTRICTS OF GRIEF: TORONTO

Alice Burdick

19 D'Arcy Street

When I was a child, I felt myself a young person in a community of older people. And later, as I grew older, I understood that they were young. There was something about this community of young people who had travelled north to escape death – dying and killing (the Vietnam War) – that felt full of potential life and creation: the children in gathering and diminishing groups, the adults in passionate discussions of political and social states. It meant that I often felt the absence of people – the whoosh in a room when a person left the group, when it was quiet for a moment in the middle of the persistent buzz of voices.

I felt even as a very young child that there was always death. I really mean this. There was constant sorrow. Where did it come from? A collection of realities. Partly, it came from my parents' frequent fights, a circuit of joy, mundane chores and screaming, tearing arguments. The hole around a child from that tension, living in that circuit, addressing daily habits in the middle of a boring maelstrom. The hole that became a cave, a blanket, a ditch, a shelter. The feeling that happiness could get sucked away in a moment. That absence was immediately and frequently possible. And not undesirable, compared to anger and fear – perhaps sometimes preferable to have absence rather than hostility. My mother's, Mary Paisley's, sorrow was tangible and frequently apparent – she was "manic-depressive" (now known as bipolar) and veered between bouts of fierce activity and severe immobility. I realized, as I got older, that she often really wanted to die, to escape her excruciating, long-seated pain. She fought that feeling, but it frequently returned, and she attempted suicide a few times in her life.

It came also from the worlds I entered when I read, and earlier, when I was read to, by my loving and distraught parents. The worlds of words contained death in the mix. The fairy tales told me a familiar story of this tilting life, how quickly the unfair descends, the flowers fade, the hidden world, sometimes bright, sometimes shadowed, leaps out to swallow the visible. This was a safe way to enter death and return. To see the future, with its beauty – love and happiness and bright sun and rolling fields and genesis – and its removal. These other worlds were also journeyed to through constant music and art that was created and made visible and audible. There were whole worlds there, ways to go through those worlds without constant continual fear of remaining in the dark. There were dark woods and fierce wolves, leaping colours and dark marks. I do feel that my childhood was full of necessary routes for escape, tools for hard times that have served me well in life.

Huron Street

These places, this feeling, came back in a recognizable way when my mother brought my brother and me to a shelter, after the final argument that became too physical. I physically escaped also as I got older – went for very long walks, uninterrupted journeys from the east end of Toronto to the west, hours and hours of walking and thinking and not thinking. I did this and skipped school, avoided home life, was entirely alone.

49 Hiawatha Road

My mother tried to kill herself on many occasions before she finally achieved her goal in August 1994. I was twenty-three years old and my brother, Brendan, had just turned seventeen. I was living in Vancouver, on Powell Street at the time, and a few days before she died someone broke into the apartment I lived in and took a random assortment of jewellery from the washroom. Some of the pieces had been given to me when I was a child, some were from my mother – they all acquired additional meaning when she died. I drew the items on little pieces of paper and described them the best I could, and I still have them. I got a phone call from my mother's friend Velvet, whom she'd met in the shelter and who'd become my mother's only constant friend. Vel told me that my mother was in the hospital, that Brendan had found her and called the ambulance, that he was with her. I got an immediate flight back to Toronto. As I flew, I knew she was dying. She had overdosed on Tylenol. She was conscious when my brother found her. As soon as I got to the Toronto airport, I went home and immediately left in a cab with my brother to what was then Toronto East General Hospital. It was late at night, after hours, and the cab driver dropped us off outside. We had to walk around the hospital until we found a way in – I experienced a mounting feeling of anxiety as we tried to find a door. It was like a locked-and-barred keep, or a maze with no entrance. When we got in, a nurse told us that she had died. She brought me in to identify my mother. This moment sunk deep into my brain and heart immediately.

The East End of Toronto holds corners and intersections of memories of my mother and her death, and the months afterwards of grief, of going through her belongings and disposing of some, keeping others, of cataloguing her artwork, of living with my brother and trying to help set up his housing. The melancholy and grief that foreshadowed her death – this projection is a frequent occurrence with the deeply depressed and suicidal, I think – joined with the fact of her death. Afterwards, when I still lived in Toronto, and later, when I've visited and end up in these places, I have recalled her end as well as other various moments of our joined lives.

The West End of Toronto holds for me the memory of Gary Côté, the boyfriend I met in 1995, a year after my mother's death. We fell deeply in love with each other that summer and spent any time we could hanging out, talking, laughing, eating, making love. He was a courier who rode hard in all weather, and I was elbow-deep in various food preparation jobs at cafés and restaurants, as well as writing poetry, and still very raw (alternating with numb) from my mother's death.

King Street West, Springhurst Avenue, The Queensway

We dated each other for a couple of years, living in different apartments. Gary fell deeply ill when I lived on Springhurst

Avenue, and was hospitalized at St. Joseph's Health Centre. After a mysterious cold that lasted way too long, his lung collapsed and there was an emergency surgery to remove part of the lung, which had deteriorated. After a few weeks in the hospital, he was diagnosed with HIV and started to take the cocktail of drugs that slowly helped contribute, along with his strong will to live, to his climb back up to health.

90 Dewson Street

We lived together in a more explicit way at 90 Dewson Street, a beautiful apartment that felt like living in a tree house, with the limbs and leaves of the surrounding maple trees a canopy over the second-floor flat and deck. I came home from work one day in October 1999 to find that he had gone. He'd been feeling a bit under the weather the previous couple of days and was at the hospital. I went to visit him there – at St. Joseph's Health Centre again. He was weak but in good spirits. His family was there, visiting him, and it seemed like he would get better. The next night I went back, after work, and snuggled with him in the hospital bed. He talked about seeing a panther, a cat in the shadows, a visitor from the spirit world. His manner was calm and clear – he seemed to be viewing things in many dimensions: the banal hospital room, and a whole other world invisible to me. He convinced me to go home and said he loved me, and I said I loved him. I remember every detail of that night. The streetcar home, the street lights on the corner of Dewson and College, feeding my old cat Ed, the phone call from Gary's mother, Bev, in the very early hours of morning telling me he had died.

Weirdly again there was a repetition of my experience from five years before, trying to get into the hospital that held the body of my loved one. There was no light on the outside of the building and I tried various doors before succeeding and going up to his room. His family stood around him, and we all tried to process his sudden removal. It felt so fast after so many years of health.

The next few months – the year really, but especially the first few months – were a disorienting time, where I eventually walked the streets of the neighbourhood, and had a startling revelation: that all the strangers walking around me, our paths crossing, had their own stories, loves, heartbreaks, losses. I didn't feel quite real myself, just a floating thing full of emotion. The streets seemed so full of stories, voices, history, that I became overwhelmed by their multiplicity. I had always enjoyed the density of the city, of the movement of people, but I suddenly had a sense of what this meant beyond the physical choreography. This sense has stayed with me. All places are full of echoes and memories, but there's something about a city that holds an almost tactile layering of these fragments.

The decades accrue, our human modus operandi. We are born, we grow in various ways, we live, we decay in various ways, we die. Time accrues, it forks out into the space of other nature. Trees, rocks, water, waterways, the gathering silt, the fishbones that break down into the undergrowth, the animals that grow and die repeatedly, along with us. Some things get left behind, though. Memories drape themselves over landmarks, small holograms of experience pop up at intersections and front porches. Invisible things that leave an impression beyond the physical world.

CEDAR DARKENING A TRAIL

Marilyn Dumont

Since the cycling accident on the Stanley Park Seawall that clipped your life short in 2016, Vancouver, with its snow-capped mountains, shining ocean and lush foliage, is now saturated with absence: where the meeting of mountains and sea was once extraordinary it is now commonplace; where great cedars towered toward the promising sun, they are now merely a stirring of a grief-tinged sky.

I moved here alone to attend UBC in 1994. The city was foreign to this prairie girl. Unfriendly, Hastings, Granville and Robson were fast-paced, expensive, mean, dismissive of someone not used to the pace, the crowd, the expense and the pollution. And those like me, a poor student who existed around its edges, feared we might be pushed even further to its fringes, like those crouched on sidewalks with their cardboard signs asking for food or shelter.

We met through the *Georgia Straight* personals. You were fifteen years my senior. I felt an affinity with you because when I spoke about my experience of racism as an Indigenous woman, you never denied it; instead you affirmed it. You had grown up in Prince Rupert, to a family of fishermen, and I had grown up in logging camps in the foothills of Alberta. You knew the physical demands of working on a fishing boat with your father, the chilling spray of the ocean and the taste of halibut and salmon, and I was familiar with the scent of sawdust and the sound of skid horses and a life of logging camps where we lived on moose or deer. We shared this experience of growing up in a working-class family surrounded by Aboriginal Peoples. I am Cree/Metis, and you had attended school and socialized with First Nations from Gitxaala, Metlakatla, Kitsumkalum and Lax Kw'alaams, Gitga'at, Haisla and Kitselas in Prince Rupert. You shared with me your attraction for Indigenous women that had developed in your teen years. I was drawn to your ability to listen, along with your love of reading and foreign films, and your disdain for racism.

Our first date was attending a Vancouver Canadians home game because you had free tickets for cheap seats, which you had picked up as some supermarket promotion. We had moved to more expensive, covered seats because so many of them seemed to be vacant, but as the game wore on and the more expensive seats began to fill, we found ourselves relinquishing our seats repeatedly to those who had purchased tickets. We laughed about our displacement and this game of musical chairs.

We likely ended the night by walking through the verdant arboretum of ponderosa pine, subalpine spruce, Douglas fir, and the Quarry Gardens rich in Japanese cherry blossoms, rhododendrons, azaleas in Queen Elizabeth Park, stopping at the viewpoint to gaze out at the North Shore mountains, the lights on Grouse and the string of city lights below.

I was unfamiliar with big city life, but as I accompanied you on walks and drives through the city to Jericho or Kitsilano Beach, over the Cambie Street Bridge to the Cinematheque or on trips to Commercial Drive for coffee, I began to learn how to navigate and feel like I belonged in that metropolis with the others who had migrated to its climate.

The ascending North Shore mountains, particularly Cypress, stalls in my mind where you used to cross-country ski. It's no longer an impressive snowy peak in which you could be found gliding over its groomed trails in winter. Instead it's the imagined cold of a deserted space in the shadow of fir and cedar darkening a trail you used to light.

The sinuous Stanley Park Seawall you cycled every morning, with its seabirds, lapping waves and joggers, once a promising destination for strolling, is now a grim pilgrimage of loneliness and longing wafting on a sea breeze. The magnolia blossoms break open only to their deaths now, and the Rose Garden spreads out funereal. Restaurants like the Naam, Sophie's Cosmic Cafe or the ChongQing are now sites of remembered shared meals and conversation, no longer available to me. Commercial Drive, Davie and Denman Streets are crowded urban spaces of bodies and unrecognizable longing, having shed their vitality and interest.

That coastal city felt home to this prairie girl in a small way because of you, but once you were gone it meant little. You gave the city meaning and significance because of your history there: raising your family in the False Creek Co-op, working at the University Hospital and cycling the seawall.

One of the last times I visited you in Vancouver, an incident evoked an epiphany for me. We were on a Vancouver city transit bus, likely going to the Cinematheque, when a couple of street people tried to slip on the bus unnoticed through the back door as others de-boarded at a stop. The driver of the bus spied them in his rear-view mirror and informed them that they would have to get off and enter through the front door where they could pay. The street people exited and walked to the front of the bus while the bus driver refused to open the front door for them and instead drove off. Ron expressed his distaste for the bus driver's actions by saying, "Well, at least you could have been kind." The bus driver responded that they had to pay like everyone else. I then spoke up and reminded the driver that "the money didn't come out of his pocket." No one else on the bus said anything, and in that moment I realized that Ron and I were kin in our shared value for social justice and advocacy for the poor.

This west coast city no longer exists as an oasis from prairie winters or social conservatism, but now abides as a site cut through with something lost, a reflection of my past.

THREE:
ELEMENTAL SPACES

ANCESTRAL WATERS

Waubgeshig Rice

Before I learned to walk, I floated in the cool waters of Georgian Bay under a brilliant sun in the summer heat. Adults and teenaged relatives took turns holding me up, keeping me buoyant with my head above water and my chubby infant legs kicking. My grandmothers also often took turns immersing me in the ancestral bay, sometimes at beaches and inlets on opposite shores. They were remarkable women with two very different backgrounds, but they were bound by their love for the water and for us, their grandchildren. Their illustrious hearts beat along with the lapping waves against the shoreline. The soothing rhythm reverberates in my own heart, even though they're no longer here.

My paternal grandmother, Aileen Rice, was born in Wasauksing First Nation and spent her entire life in the Anishinaabe community. It's a large rocky and green island on Georgian Bay, adjacent to Parry Sound, Ontario. We called her Grandma, or Nokomis. My maternal grandmother, Ruth Shipman, grew up in Kapuskasing, Ontario, and she and my grandfather moved their family to Parry Sound when my mother was a teen. We called her Grannie. Both women were beautiful and radiant constants in our lives. As formidable matriarchs, they raised us all to be kind and respectful to others, and to the land and water around us.

Their spirited legacies flow through our blood and in the currents and waves of Georgian Bay. They each died of natural causes less than a year apart. My Grannie, my mom's mom, died in June 2017, as the summer was about to get underway. She was ninety-two. My Grandma, my dad's mom, died the following February, at the peak of winter. She was about to turn eighty-seven. The water warmed for one's journey and froze over for the other's. The duality of their deaths was emblematic of their lives and the disparate communities from which they came: an Indigenous woman from the rez and a white woman from town.

Losing both of my grandmothers in such a short time was devastating. It took me a long time to properly grieve their deaths. To many, a grandmother is larger than life; a family's grand matriarch who leads and holds everything together. I was fortunate to have two such powerful women as influential forces in my life. They taught me almost everything – from how to swim to how to love. Most importantly, they instilled in me the strongest sense of family and those around me, *all connected* to the land and water that nurtured us.

Their paths ran parallel in almost opposite realms, and finally intersected when my parents got together. It was a bond that became stronger upon my arrival in this world. Both families grew close thanks to celebrations and gatherings in homes on the rez and in town. My cousins on either side began calling each other cousins. Love transcended cultural, racial and socio-economic differences because of the example set by these two powerful matriarchs. Our families regularly gathered near the summer waters of Georgian Bay, marking birthdays and other special occasions, and often just the joy of the season. Summers at either grandmother's beach are some of my fondest memories.

As soon as the weather warmed, my Grandma stayed in a cabin near a beach on the reserve in what's known as "Waubgeshig's Cove" – a tiny inlet named after her father (whose name I've come proudly to bear). It's where her parents took her and her ten siblings in the summertime beginning in the 1920s. She kept that family connection alive as her own children, including my father, grew up in the Anishinaabe way. It was her favourite place. She cherished the black sand of the beach and large rocks that bookended it. She revered the large pine, oak and birch trees that sheltered the beach and her cabin. She could proudly trace her lineage deep into the mainland, across the water in what is now the town of Parry Sound.

Around the point, to the east of my Grandma's beach and across the water on the mainland, my Grannie had her own Georgian Bay refuge. They moved to the area in the early 1970s because my grandfather had bought a marina on the outskirts of Parry Sound. They eventually put a trailer on the far side of the property, where a tiny beach was similarly nestled between big grey rocks under a thick canopy of trees. She stayed there all summer long every year. It was her own favourite place. Georgian Bay wasn't originally a part of her family's heritage, but she made it so.

Although they shared a similar passion for the water, my grandmothers came to be on Georgian Bay via quite contrasting courses. One was born just steps from the shore, speaking a language that long predated the formation of the society eventually imposed upon her family and community. It was a ruling order that forbade that language and traditional way of life in violent ways. The other came to the area following an opportunity to plant roots in hopes of enabling subsequent generations to thrive. The water separated them physically: Grandma on the island reserve and Grannie in town. But love and dedication to family brought them together. It's a nurturing spirit of home and kin that's pulsed through the bay itself for millennia.

Among many of the Anishinaabeg who've lived on and near its shores for innumerable generations, Georgian Bay is known as "Manidoo gaming," or "spirit lake." It was always considered a very powerful and spiritual body of water. Tales of epic migrations, historic gatherings and ethereal phenomena connected to Manidoo gaming have echoed through Anishinaabe history. I've been fortunate to hear some of these stories since I was a child. They've connected me to the land and water in the most profound ways, bolstering the pride that was already in my DNA. My Grandma always made sure to nurture that. So did my Grannie.

The ancestral waters are still revered by the communities that currently surround them, albeit in different ways due to varying histories. The people who traditionally traversed the shorelines and paddled the inlets and open bay were forced onto smaller pockets of so-called "reserved" land by the authorities who created what is now known as Canada. The European descendants who settled towns around the bay were then able to exploit the land's natural resources and sustain viable, thriving communities. Meanwhile, across the bay, the Anishinaabeg struggled as their traditional way of life withered. It took a long time for our community to reconnect with the medicine of the old ways, but now many people are on a path to healing.

Our families walked together on that path. Our grandmothers led the way. They cared deeply for one another until the end, each asking regularly about her counterpart when the tolls of old age rendered in-person visits impossible. Theirs was a living example of wholesome and respectful relationship-building that the ruling orders, and society in general, have long failed to accomplish or neglected outright. It's a journey that continues even though both of them have left us.

But the lapping waves on the shores will echo their beating hearts for as long as we're around to hear the water's rhythmic pulse along the sand and rocks. Their spirits are in the water and in us. My grandmothers made sure we had a place in this historic and beautiful territory. We honour them by thriving here, and protecting what's been passed down since time immemorial. The grief lingers, but softens with each freeze-up and thaw of the mighty Georgian Bay. That initial sorrow has made way for celebration and pride. My grandmothers have never left. We swim in their ancestral waters, safe in their embrace.

HOW THE RIVER SWELLS

Canisia Lubrin

My best friend died in the Roseau River, so I know it well enough. Amid the sprawling bamboo and the banana groves of Saint Lucia's west coast, the sonic madness of the Roseau River scars its course in the short distance between the mountains and the Caribbean Sea at Roseau Beach. I know it as a place of great reverie, too. It was where my brother taught me how to swim one summer of our childhood in the late 1980s. Hold your breath, stretch out like you're lying down on your belly, rotate your arms like propellers, kick the water like you know how to do football tricks. But being a young boy, as I imagined all young boys to be – cavalier and performative – my brother and his swimming lessons graduated quickly away from me and my water skill set. And because I, usually the only girl in the gang, did not want to seem weak or incapable, I was front-flipping off the top of that embankment, with the spotty patches of grass and the feet-beaten stair-like mud tracks leading down to the basin where most villagers did their laundry, as soon as I felt a morsel of bravery. After several trips to the river that saw me walk away from my own near-drownings, from being disoriented after coughing out a little water and then a lot of water from my lungs, from wishing myself pairs of new eyes after trying to keep mine open underwater for too long thinking this would improve my chances of swimming like I meant it, I met with a vanishing point one Monday morning in September 1989. Before my brother's patience waned completely, I had learned to swim better and started to value the cost of finding myself improved. I began to swim well enough to almost keep up with the rest of the boys.

My best friend throughout my earliest years in Saint Lucia's Roseau Valley was also my niece. We were just four years apart in age and were inseparable, and even as I look back from here, my three decades-plus life, I see her as she was on many days: running around the yard, her whole head a shrieking laughter, hibiscus pinned above her ear and tucked in her hair, sucking on a chicken bone with her oily mouth, singing her own lyrics to Elton John's "Sacrifice." My sister, my niece's mother, kept her eyes on us, it seemed, even though she had to leave us in someone's care while she ran an errand or two. She knew everything we did while she was away. She knew things. But when my niece, her daughter, died that September, she seemed unaware that she herself was still alive. She had died with my niece in everything but her own body, which was slowly disappearing, ravaged by grief. Other things I remember about my niece's death come to me unexpectedly now and then, a child learning grown-up things, a grown-up learning grown-up things. And the memories I offer you now have been blank pages unsure of so much, things still strange to me, things with no home, no place to begin or conclude. Things only I am aware are waiting for me. They're my haunt and they come in flashbacks of the river, the yard, the coconut tree on the side of the road that I stood beneath and waited and waited for what seemed like an entire year.

September 1989. I leave home for school and tell my niece to expect me back as soon as school is over, and we will go fruit picking in the backyard and we will "sell" these fruits to our dogs and the cat and the chickens. This is the thing we loved to do. I leave the classroom with the rest of my schoolmates and pour into the schoolyard at the last bell. It had rained briefly that noon hour and the ground beneath the fierce early afternoon sun was now dry, but, in the nose, evidence of that drizzle lingered like a spell, the air still smelling of hot wet coals. As I walk down the grey pavement at the entrance of the compound, and as the bazaar-like buzz of chattering children dies out behind me, I hear a wail. A wail as guttural as it is operatic, but which amuses me, so I laugh before the woman who owns the sound appears in the periphery of my vision. She wears a red cloth around her waist, bunched up with the excesses of her flared dress on her hip. She wears a checkered mouchwè: yellow, red, black, green, brown. She flails her arms and I hear her say my mother's name. I hear her say that my mother's granddaughter has drowned at the river. I hear her keep on her wailing. My heart jumps into my mouth and I swallow. I run and catch up with the woman who keeps up with her wailing and her news report all at once, and thread through the main road screaming at her: *Which Monica? Which Monica?* She does not seem to hear me. Before long, I am back up the hill near the house at the side of the main road. I am standing beneath a tall coconut tree looking into our yard, which is still, if not windless.

The house by its quiet, its solitude, its subdued space seems to confirm something of what the woman had been screaming. *Which Monica?* My mother. I am afraid to go close to the house. I did not trust its unpeopled state. I am five years old and panicked, so I walk back to the coconut tree and stand beneath it. I soon realize that our house is not the only unpeopled house. I stand, place my backpack on the wild roots of the coconut tree veining beneath my feet and wait.

Hours pass. I find no way to translate this sorrow I felt beyond feeling suddenly ripped open. Grave and quiet. Dark. So, when a coconut falls from the tree and hits me on the head, my neighbour, a cognitively impaired, shy and gentle young man who lives in the pink house next to the coconut tree comes over to me, smiling, and tells me that my niece has drowned and there is nobody home and that everyone has forgotten about me. I yell at him, frustrated and in pain, and ask him to leave me alone. Soon some women pass me bending into the shadow of the coconut tree and say, *poor little child poor her poor them*, looking at me and then off into the sunset across the valley. I dislike these women for thinking they understand anything that is happening to me, especially because I do not understand any of it myself. The horizon glows red. I feel myself growing afraid even of the sun. But then I realize that it is not the fear of the sun that is my affliction but the pending darkness and the uncertainty that anyone would ever return home. And even if they returned, would they return with the absence I newly feared?

One evening in Toronto, I decide that I have had enough of the Discovery Channel: no more of these documentaries about flamingos feeding on pink shrimp, hummingbirds' impossible locomotion and prehistoric leatherbacks beaching their semi-doomed eggs. No more of these picturesque, difficult things narrated in beautiful British accents. *What about the people of the Antilles, not the beasts*, I mumble at the documentary. In those words, I recognized grief. I had spent several hours that day trying to compose a poem about my niece for a repeating line creative writing assignment. The instructions included writing about something difficult. I thought I knew enough about myself to imagine I could write this thing twenty-two years removed. Later that night, I finally wrote the poem. And then I wept. Truly wept for my niece for the first time that I remember. And I wonder if I have avoided having a best friend since because I never really mourned her. Too many reminders that this could be true. Too many forces suggesting miracles.

It has been decades since I saw my sister elbow deep in mud. Surely I can fend off this estrangement: no to that pending revelation, no to that form of dying – one without the understanding that we are supposed to know loss and know it intimately. It has been decades since I started writing stories about that great loss, since I decided to keep my niece's place in my heart for only her. I have kept friends at arm's length and met other losses with those same outstretched arms. I did not know that grief would make me a writer.

> I'm thinking of writing a book, I told my sister.
> She said, "If you must write, then by every means, write."
> I felt very little persuasion at those words.

August 2007. As I walked to the base of that same hill where my sister had laid in complete surrender to death and wept,

I could hear music lamenting from the Church of the Holy Family. I was no longer a believer, but I loved the familiar theatre of certain rituals – the parts of the mass that my niece had loved to sing. So why not enter it now that I knew for sure where I stood in whatever faith I had chosen? How the years churn out their meaning, how the good fortune of certain memories have made me soft. I had come to associate that church with the child who'd decided to just run rampant and have a grand time interrupting mass the day before she died. I dip my fingers in the little gold dish of holy water out of respect. The priest was in the middle of a sermon, about which I can say nothing specific, though I do remember not being particularly interested. And then sudden darkness. And then I am floating down a river. And then that river suddenly becomes cloud, bright white, and I am face to face with a cherub. Smiling, her whole head a shriek of laughter, singing her own lyrics to Elton John's "Sacrifice," sucking on a chicken bone with her oily mouth. I reach out for her and before I can touch her, I wake up.

A woman is above me as my vision un-blurs, fanning me madly with a prayer pamphlet. I wrestled myself out of the woman's arms, made my way out of the church, out of breath. Save for a few steps I actually remember, I was barely conscious when I entered my father's house, a few houses southeast of the church. The church, which stands on Jacmel Hill, from whose yard you hear the river, its mad gushing loudest on rainy days.

June 1999. On the lone windowsill in my father's kitchen rests an ornate wood-carved picture frame in which a piece of matted cotton rag depicts, in watercolour, these words: *truth is, we've all been framed*. I reach for it and hold it to my breast, and a piece of paper falls out from the back. I pick it up and look at it. It is a black and white picture, almost completely faded, but I am sure I make out at least a partial hint of a face and a coffin laden with faded flowers. We are not close, my father and I. And even as I think I've seen this picture before and try to ask him about it, I seem unable to speak clearly.

At a loss for what else to do, I turn around to walk away, imagining that our father was almost reaching out to stop me. You look familiar, he'd say to me, if he was attentive long enough.

I scan the front door and slowly walk through it and into his yard.

I imagine him saying, if you are leaving can you wave bye-bye.

Someday, someone will ask who was in that picture and I will say, *My niece, my best friend*.

I own no photographs of this river that took her, but I see it clearly in my dreams. It is legendary for swelling without warning. *Rain. From the mountains*, my brother might still remind me today.

PLANET GRIEF

Christine Lowther

My glen of the star-tangled yews,
where hares would lope in the easy dew.
To remember is a ringing pain of brightness.
– "Deirdre Remembers a Glen"

I am not reconciled with the kind of love deep enough to end
by killing. Is it like knowing you're going down so you raze
a precious woodland to the ground? Is it the same as paving
over a sweet meadow with cement?

My sister is nine; I am seven going on eight. Our parents
introduce us to a wondrous parallel universe, opposite to
Vancouver's siren-serenaded bedtimes and traffic-choked
streets. We drive through a black hole (the George Massey
Tunnel) and board a ferry that carries us through Active Pass.
Driving off the vessel onto Mayne Island with car windows
down, we smell wild Nootka rose – not its blooms but its
foliage. Summers are crispy-dry. We see – or sense or imagine
or hear – arbutus bark peeling from contorted trunks. We
are looking. We are listening. The scraps of bark will snap

underfoot, break in our fists. Winters are damp and green. Wooden docks will always lead us to and away from this place, where beaches are arrived at through trees and over grass.

SOCIAL WORKER'S REPORT

We were contacted at home on the evening of October 20, 1975, by Sgt. James F—, RCMP, General Section, Vancouver, who advised us that he had very deep concerns as to the safety of the a/n children on Mayne Island.

Sgt. F— informed us that he was one of the officers investigating the murder of Mrs. Patricia Lowther and that he had travelled to Victoria for the purpose of officially notifying the Dept of Human resources of his concerns for the girls' safety. It appeared that the investigation was leading to a definite possibility that their father would be arrested and charged with the murder.

The island is a galaxy of loving relatives, open fields, beaches, forests of conifers and arbutus. But this time it is grey, cold and foreboding. He brings us in the darkness and our mother is absent. He lies to us, says she went away, as if she would ever go without saying goodbye. Our once-magical parallel universe is now our hideaway. He is running. Sand and rocks hide scuttling crabs until we expose them with our hands.

The investigating officers believe that the father expects imminent arrest and that there is a definite possibility that he might kill the girls and commit suicide. Further discussion convinced us that their concerns were real. Arrangements were made to meet Sgt. F— and Detective Ben E. S— of the Vancouver City Police Homicide Division, the other investigating officer on the Mayne Island aspects of the murder, on the morning of October 21, 1975, at our Sidney Office.

Because of the inconvenient ferry schedule to Mayne Island, we requested the assistance of the RCMP patrol boat and obtained full co-operation. We also solicited the assistance of Social Worker Allison W— from Saanich DHR office after discussing the particulars of the case with D/S Luke M—.

During our discussions with the investigating officers, they both noted that their conclusions were formed in part by the father's very deep love for the girls. They further noted that they were unable to anticipate the reactions of the father were he to be advised of the apprehension of his children.

Is this the kind of love deep enough to end by poisoning a rare wetland? Or is it more like sawing through a favourite tree and pushing it over, making sure you're underneath when it falls?

On arriving at Mayne Island, the officers were in contact with the Vancouver Police Offices but could not obtain permission to arrest the father. They indicated that they were awaiting lab reports or other corroborating evidence before they would receive orders to arrest.

The circumstances here left Allison W— and the writer in the position of approaching a man who was expecting to be charged with murder, and advising him that we must apprehend his children for their protection. If the man was taken into custody, we could have simply lodged the girls with interested and concerned relatives on Mayne Island; whereas, if he were not arrested, we then would have to remove them of [sic] Mayne Island for their protection.

Consideration was given to the possibility of waiting overnight for the arrest, but the officers were unable to anticipate when their instructions would arrive. The officers promised to stay close by during any conversations with the father.

After days of building tension, our father pacing in the tiny cabin, words are ejected, unadorned: "Your mother's dead." We cry, not asking how or when. Yet the tears soon stop, followed by a heavy silence. What now? "I'm over it," I say. "*I'm* not over it," says my older sister. I am ashamed. As long as he is still present, life is bearable to me, still feels safe. He has purposefully moulded a daddy's girl.

At the time we decided we must proceed with the apprehension without father's arrest, his car disappeared from in front of his cabin. We awaited his return until about 2:00 p.m., when one of the officers found his car parked some distance away at a secluded cove.

We had already learned that the children were at school. We obtained the assistance of a maternal [great-]aunt, Mrs. Elsie Wilks, and her daughter-in-law, Mrs. Vera Wilks. Both ladies agreed to go to the school with us to support the girls and briefly explain the apprehension.

We therefore decided that we must apprehend the girls at the school and advise the father later of our actions. The teacher agreed to have them in her office without anyone else being aware of the situation.

Children of all grades are taught in a single classroom. Behind the school is another forest leading to another field; we could be happy here. But the whole island knows he is a suspect before we do. A classmate calls across the playground to my sister: "Hey! Heard your mother's dead. Heard your father killed her." A girl throws a rock at my face. We are surrounded. "Why aren't you crying?" becomes a chant.

When the children were picked up, the two Mrs. Wilks, Allison and the writer proceeded to the police boat. The girls were left in Allison's care while the writer went to advise the father, in the company of Sgts. F— and Creakley. We found Mr. Lowther at the secluded waterfront spot where we had a twenty- to thirty-minute conversation with him. It is enough to say that it was a very unpleasant task without further details, except that he expressed some hostility amid much weeping and anguish. When he composed himself somewhat, he was able to give us the names of relations who he wished to assist and in the order in which they should be contacted. After further control of his emotions, Mr. Lowther agreed to accompany us to see his daughters. He retained his composure very well in the presence of the girls and simply explained that it would be best for them to go with us for a short while as he was going to be busy.

Why has the social worker lied? Because he didn't want his superiors to know? The pathetic scene of crying, clinging and begging between father and daughters is a memory that

I bury deep underground, where it will stay until one winter night when I am in my mid-twenties. During a leadership training program called Wilderness of Women, surrounded by several other earnest young women, the memory will raise its head, sniff the air, feel the safety and surface. My friends will hold onto me as I sob into a pillow to muffle the sound. The "recovered memory" will appear like this: *The police and detectives, voices raised, are pressuring us to separate; they might even be pulling at our arms. The father's voice, swollen with sobs, cries, "Let me say goodbye to my children!" as we cling crying to him.*

Nobody says, "I know you feel horrible. I'm sorry for what is happening. We are taking you to a nice family with children your age." Or if they do, it leaves no brainwaves.

Abuse victims' recovered memories will be a psychological trend in the '90s, leading to some false accusations and panic; they will later be challenged and even, as some say, debunked. Clifton Crais will write in his 2014 book *History Lessons*: "The crystalline, lucid image of a traumatic experience is not perfectly accurate, though it feels that way. Flashbulb memories are no complete replica within the human mind of what happened. They can be inaccurate, and they exact a certain cost. The very same cortisol that helps create flashbulb memories also destroys neurons, quite literally obliterating memory surrounding the traumatic experience. A likeness exists as if it were a photograph, but shorn of its surroundings." It could be that our father is the only one crying. It could be that my sister is the only one not crying. That isn't how I remember it. How I remember it might not be *the* history, but it is *a* history. Mine. It is the last time I ever see my father.

The accused, standing on the dock, recedes to an ink smudge, never to be seen again. We move away over water. Dock shrinking. Him, dwindling, disappearing. *To remember is a ringing pain of brightness.*

. . . He retained his composure very well in the presence of the girls and simply explained that it would be best for them to go with us for a short while as he was going to be busy. . . .

If this is retaining composure, he must have been hysterical when they accosted him in that secluded cove.

A short while: the rest of our lives without our mum or dad.

Busy: being arrested and charged.

Busy getting bailed out by a *girlfriend.*

Busy being found guilty of second-degree murder despite evidence of first-degree murder.

As busy as his secret history spent in Riverview psychiatric institution, long before he met Mum – his second wife. Pat. Her name was Pat.

As busy as his attempt to strangle the first wife, Hannah, witnessed by two of their children.

A dock is a place of coming and going. It is a transitional finger that points from water to land, and from land to water. For me, Miners Bay dock represents a tearing away from my remaining parent to severance, orphaning, confusion, grief, fear, mortification, shame, guilt, loneliness, anchorlessness. Loss. The very stars change position. This all sounds very dramatic. That's exactly what it is. A shaking of the soul. Life defining, Dickensian tragedy.

I am bound to the memory of a particular field. Right outside the cabin called Sleepy Hollow that we stay in, it's the pale turf we traverse to access the beach. In 2000, I'll write of being a child with my family, freed from the city, with "the ultimate freedom to run through the long, dry grass and over the short bank onto the sand." As otherworldly to me as Narnia in my favourite book series, a land inconsistently accessed through a wardrobe, with its own time: the field can reveal astounding things, host remarkable events in the cosmos.

A child obsessed with deer, I happen to be looking out the window one morning in Sleepy Hollow. Great-uncle Bill is running, clapping his hands, chasing an antlered buck out of the apple orchard. The buck leaps beautifully over the fence, sprints across the field and into the forest of arbutus and Douglas fir.

I don't return to Mayne Island until my late teens, long after Auntie Elsie has passed on. I can only feel pleasure, wonder and welcome familiarity whizzing by Miners Bay dock on a bicycle en route to the lighthouse, where more of my relatives live. The memory hasn't surfaced yet. My high school friend and I visit the eccentric great-uncle and hike around his property, formerly that of the Canadian government, which sold it to him for about ten dollars. Land inhabited by Coast Salish peoples for 8,000 years. Uncle Bill has written a book called *Science of a Witch's Brew*. He lets us hold homemade divining wires that swivel and point, he tells us, to where we were born. Years later, when Bill dies, his land goes up for sale – a terrifying prospect until it is purchased by the federal government, and added to Gulf Islands National Park Reserve (Bennett Bay).

In the summer of 1991, after many years abroad, I find the trees hauntingly quiet, the grass empty of children and deer. Journal entry:

Today I sat on a cliff in the rain, staring across the high tide toward the beloved field where the old wizard, Gram's brother Bill, lived. . . . I sat missing him and my mother, and feeling how this island misses them, still mourns their loss, five and sixteen years gone respectively. Maybe those two seals I spotted were Uncle Bill and Auntie Elsie. The heron was Mother, graceful and cautious. . . . Yesterday, I went wandering, barefoot. I wanted to hug the rocky, mossy ground, crunch-step in the leaves, climb the arbutus trees – but I just cried and cried. Every time I thought I was finished and started to head back to the tent, I'd start again. I was mourning for the dead, for those left alive, for my childhood, and for finally being in places I've long dreamed of revisiting. I'm actually here . . . This is not a dream. Near our tent lies a decayed remnant of a chipmunk. Its tiny paw waves in the wind. And when I was walking along in tears, a chipmunk scrambled up a branch over my head, scolding, very much alive.

Grieving takes a lot of energy. Could I accomplish this work if the land were developed rather than left wild? Maybe through guided meditation or visualization (or a holodeck, if you're a Star Trek fan). But I'll have better mental health thanks to wild spaces. I'll know the deer and woodpeckers haven't had to give up their homes. I do wonder if the land misses its First Peoples, with their seasonal fish-following villages. Some change can be desirable, like putting things back the way they were.

I will return to the island one autumn in my forties. Sleepy Hollow will be long gone. At the field a new sign will read: "Parks Canada and the Mayne Island Conservancy Society are working together on the ecological restoration of this site. To return the area to its natural state, native trees have been planted. The cages protect the young saplings from deer browsing. PLEASE DO NOT REMOVE THE CAGES." The grass will be dotted with many caged trees. Even though I've always been pro-forest, I will email Mayne Island Conservancy to ask why the meadow has to go.

The reply will satisfy me. Mayne Island has less than 5 percent of its land permanently protected as parkland, the lowest of any island in the Islands Trust area. Reforesting the open field will increase habitat for native plants and animals, and shade-out the many invasive species growing there now. I will have wandered among the cages, looking down into them, my tears watering their occupants. They belong here; they will grow well. "Grief offers a wild alchemy that transmutes suffering into fertile ground," Francis Weller writes in his book, *The Wild Edge of Sorrow*. The field lived with invasives for decades, perhaps centuries, and will now be allowed to support new life. I will have lived with invasive events most of my life. Restoration is in order.

As their root systems expand, the young trees will continue to heal erosion on the bank along the beach. Bennett Bay is located in the Coastal Douglas Fir Biogeoclimatic zone, which is one of the most threatened collections of ecosystems in Canada. The cages will contain Douglas firs and Garry oaks, among other native trees. The oaks were more omnipresent in the days of the Coast Salish. This regrowth will feel like bringing love back to the land.

During a span of two and a half years, my last three Mayne Island blood relatives will be gone. My second-cousin Barry Wilks, son of Bill and Elsie, will die suddenly in January 2015. Next, his sister Tracey will pass away. Finally, one summer my cousin Steve will move off-island. An era will be over, but the spouses of the deceased will remain. Barry's widow Sally will continue to be family to us. For someone who does not own a car, the Gulf Islands are not easy to reach. They will often feel like a distant, beckoning alternate plane of reality. Mayne Island will remain a location of past anguish to me, but no more than one of love and longing. At fifty I will wonder if the field was, in part, a wound we walked and ran on. To heal it with trees would be a rare miracle.

When I ask myself, "What or where is a grief-location?" I think of our world as a whole. Then my particular history will curl up, at least for the moment, like a thin red peel of arbutus bark. *The Wild Edge of Sorrow* speaks of a "deepening sense of loss we are feeling as the life systems of our planet show continuing signs of strain and decline. This pain is intense and almost unendurable." I will feel that pain every day, most often pushing it away. One evening, during a discussion on environmental concerns with a friend, she will blurt out: "Humans are not a cancer, we belong here. We come from planet Earth." And the words will spill from my mouth: "What if we come from grief?" And she will say, wide-eyed, "Then we need to feel that."

WATER & STONE

Catherine Graham

They mined the rock. Pipe staked. Dynamite stuffed. Limestone chunked out as giant building blocks. 1898. A man in coveralls stares at the camera lens.

In the black and white photo, he holds my stare.

My father thinks the house beside the water-filled limestone quarry will heal my mother (though I don't know this yet). They aren't looking for a new home. They love the Upside-Down house in Grimsby, backing onto the Niagara Escarpment. Kitchen upstairs, bedrooms down. A place to raise me, their little girl.

But the quarry in Ridgeway beckons.

A lump is opposite to a quarry. It's a form that pushes out, not in.

They dynamited the rock and dug into the buried world. They laid tracks at the bottom to carry the rocks out. Workhorses shouldered the weight. A working world in the basement of the Earth. The men were surrounded by stone, their hands calloused by it. Their dreams, too. The cracking of stone, smashed and blasted. It rang through their nocturnal exhaustion. At night, lying in their makeshift cots, they were too tired to take their boots off.

The water holds our family's many moods. My mother likes it calm. She likes to see the word beneath, the stillness doubling, that hinge of illusion. My father likes it rough with whitecaps, the frothy arcs that come and go; what motion cannot hold. I navigate between the two, the need to please them both. They are keeping a secret from me. I feel it in the quarry of my bones.

They are sitting in the family room that looks out on the quarry. The *Merck Manual* is tucked in the swan-curve of my mother's legs. My father is resting his hands on his forehead, elbows on his knees. He's sitting in the Windsor chair. I clutch my binder to my chest, flatten what's barely there.

"It's cancer, isn't it?"

Silence roars whitecaps in the dry room.

The working pit the men have worked so hard to mine slowly fills with water, an underground pool is released and the hidden spring seeps up and up, filling the limestone basin. The water rises like a bath, drowning the tools, the machinery.

Can horses swim? Did the men get out in time?

A blue oval is a blue eye.

Adolescence is rapid growth. The sprouting of limbs, the filling out of breasts.

Cancer is rapid growth. The removal of breast, the crippling of limbs.

My mother sits on the dock to watch me swim back and forth to the floating raft. We know she can't save me if I were to drown. That hinge of illusion.

Her cigarette smoke, a rope from her lips, slowly disappears.

The desire to die beside her beloved quarry does not happen. Pneumonia forces her into a local hospital.

Snow falls that Christmas Day. It flakes the outline of her leaving.

A gust blows it away.

When does a landscape of loss become a landscape of found?

Dad thought the quarry would heal him, too. He sits on the dock looking out to a future he can't see. Steeped in grief. He sips his beer. *Just one more before I head out.* He can't keep track. *Shuffle off to Buffalo. Watch another baseball game at a bar.* En route over the Peace Bridge I imagine him seeing the line of quarried rock extracted from our property so long ago. It protects the land along the edge of the American city, limestone mined for the Buffalo breakwater. Stone pushes water. Water holds stone. Grief pushes pain. Pain holds grief. The quarry becomes a vessel for pain.

She's gone. My Rusty.

A band of sunlight, the colour of her hair, the sun's red blade.

There's a 3:00 a.m. knocking on my bedroom door. Do I open it?

"I'm sorry to have to tell you this," says the police officer standing in the half dark.

The quarry is cold autumn blue. It's preparing for its annual lid. Up and over and back into itself.

Another soul leaves a body. It evaporates into a cloud of whitecaps.

What to do with a quarry that can't hold me anymore?

University graduate, summa cum laude, despite the weight of grief pulling me down, down.

The home that was meant to heal must be sold.

It is time to let the quarry go.

No plan to be a writer, but somehow words find me. They coat my grief and give loss a shape, a way out. The pit inside me fills with the water of words. A place to swim, to float, not drown.

And when I leave the quarry, it stays inside me. Always.

EVIL IN MY POCKET

Nikki Reimer

There's a print tacked to the wall beside my writing desk by Albertan singer/songwriter/artist Clinton St. John. I first met him nearly a decade ago over email, when I wrote to ask if I could crib a couple of his lyrics for a poem, but like many folks I know in Calgary, he's my friend now because he loved you.

The print is a black ink drawing of a large mason jar. In the bottom of the jar, sharks, fish, a jellyfish and a human body swim past sea vegetables and rocks. In the top portion is a sheet of ice, with a log cabin, some trees and a bearded lumberjack ice-fishing down into the sea. He's hooked an enormous human heart on his line.

The print is titled, *On this Cold Lake.*

We are always travelling through the arterial mountain roads from Calgary to the pretty town nestled on the eastern shore of the Okanagan Lake. When we're younger, the trip is in a four-door maroon Oldsmobile where we have to share leg space in the back seat. Then our parents upgrade to a silver minivan with double benches, and finally a purple minivan with captain's chairs. When we're preteen and teenager, we travel in style, each lost in our own Walkman or Discman, tossing bags of chips back and forth over the seats, hands getting greasy, feet up on the windows, though sometimes we'll all four of us sing our way through the entire Beatles catalogue. You like to throw things at me over the seat when I'm not looking because it makes me squawk.

We're the family that always travels together.

A month or so after you die, a friend brings me a mix-CD of grief songs, including a track called "Love Is All" by singer-songwriter Kristian Matsson, whose stage name is The Tallest Man on Earth. The song breaks me open, which takes me to the YouTube video, which breaks me open further. The lyrics of the song could be about disposing of a lover's remains, or disposing of a physical will or document, but I read it as the song's speaker letting go of a loved one's ashes in a river. I admit, though, my reading is coloured by the video: it starts like an old film reel, flickering. A mountain highway, a family. Grainy. Could be found footage. Sepia-toned saccharine nostalgia. Highway driving and snow-capped mountains on the horizon. Matsson's voice is slightly gravelly and lilting, reminiscent of Dylan but more melodic. "Evil's in my pocket and your will is in my hand. . . . And I'll throw it in the current that I stand upon so still." The video is framed like a video projector on a wall in a dark room. Is it a family vacation home movie? A series of them? The people change. Women in semi-beehive hairdos of the '60s wearing short shorts. Or maybe the '70s? Some of the men are in Speedos. A kid playing in a boat. A pretty young woman with a pixie cut. A little blond boy with a bucket marches through a parking lot toward the beach, and it's you marching through the parking lot toward the beach, and I can't handle the loss of my adult best friend but the simultaneous loss of the little boy you used to be ruptures my sternum wide open and I'm standing holding my own intestines and entrails are dripping red and bloody to the floor. "Well I walk upon the river like it's easier than land / Evil's in my pocket and your strength is in my hand." A red paddle boat bobs on sparkling lake water. The sun dances in ripples on the waves.

"And I'll throw you in the current that I stand upon so still."

Is the evil in the pocket the loved one's ashes? And the loved one's strength that must be channelled to complete the scattering in the river? I think so. It *is* evil, what's become of you, from kind and humble young man to a collection of ashes parsed out to your closest friends, the biggest in a stupid marble urn on top of our parents' piano. Evil and inexplicable reality that we are forced to confront constantly. I listen to the song several times a day for weeks, months, and I weep every time – from catharsis, from nostalgic ache, from the knowledge of what I'm going to have to do.

Matsson's voice hits a cracked pitch: "Here come the tears / But like always, I let them go." Like Pavlov's emo chick, I cry every time.

Dido wasn't great about saving money or staying in one job very long, so in 1990, he and Baba sold their house and sports cars (his, a gold Cadillac; hers a white '68 Thunderbird convertible – yeah they were lower-middle class, but the man loved his cars) and headed for the interior, where it was cheaper to live, and where he'd plan to work for ten years and retire at the age of seventy. He already had the persistent cough.

They bought a mobile home in Westbank, across the lake from Kelowna, in the same trailer park off Highway 97 where Grandma and Tony settled some months later. Were there two good summers, or only one? I don't remember. He joined a barbershop quartet, got a job at a camera store, died within the same year that the lung cancer travelled to his lymph nodes and brain. But Baba stayed. She had her Ukrainian church and her church ladies, her tidy double-wide trailer in the shadow of Mount Boucherie, her cherry trees and her TV news schedule. She had a waiting plot beside him at Kelowna Memorial Park Cemetery, a lush spot on a hill overlooking the city, though she wouldn't join him for another sixteen years.

So, for the next decade and a half, it was an eight-hour drive each way for ten to fourteen days every summer, and sometimes Thanksgiving and Easter, too. You and I in shorts and flip-flops, playing the organ in the living room, our thighs sticking to the vinyl bench, or semi-comatose on the green La-Z-Boy recliners while we watched cartoons and MuchMusic for hours. Everything SPF 30, tropical and heady, the white sweat that pools in the creases of elbows and knees. Or throwing a ball around in the open green space behind the row of trailers, or biking the circuitous route of the park. You were four when I was ten, six when I was twelve. Your hair was long and blond, which sometimes made old ladies think you were a girl. At the beach we were fish, swimming 'til our skin puckered. I would swim alone to the buoys marking the boundary of the "safe" area, loving the strength of my muscles and savouring independence. You would stay in the water 'til you shivered and your lips turned blue, your delicate long lashes stuck together, framing your sea-blue eyes. We would hug you in a towel and rub your arms and legs 'til you warmed up.

After you die, Mom will feel this small and delicate in my arms.

After you die, I start a grief-Tumblr that fills up with cartoon skeletons, grainy hipstagram photos of wildlife, stylized skulls and rage. The "Love Is All" video makes it onto a post along with pictures from the only apartment you ever lived in away from Mom and Dad. A burst of trees out your window; your windowsill on which you'd placed a piece of driftwood and old photos of our two dead grandfathers in small antique frames; a mug of forest-green matcha tea in the cupholder of your car. Grandpa John died when our dad was eighteen, and you were only six when Dido passed, but these men are important to you. There's a way we are both shaped by the lives and deaths of each man, something indelible passed through the bones that we both feel and know.

As caption, I write, "Your window, your windowsill, your car."

A dancer we know is inspired by my post and choreographs a duet in homage to me and your girlfriend, set to the song. Two young women dance together and apart on a stage that is bare except for an empty wooden chair. Sometimes one of them sits on it to rest her head in her hands. When they roll downstage, turn to it in unison and sigh, a glacial crack erupts from the centre of my ribcage as a sob bursts forth. I don't even know it's my sound 'til it's already hanging in the air. My lip trembles for the entire four minutes and sixteen seconds of the piece as I fight to stay silent.

Jonathon and I have no money and no jobs, so we pack our things and our cats into a U-Haul and head east out of Vancouver, back to Calgary. Passing through Westbank, I start narrating. "This strip mall wasn't there before. There was never a Starbucks on this side of the lake. Uncle Mike liked to go to this antique auction. Goodbye, Baba's house. Goodbye, Grandma's house. Goodbye, paintball. Goodbye, liquor store."

"Baby, what are you doing?"

"Saying goodbye to my childhood."

He takes my hand in his.

We'd started travelling to Kelowna for the summer even before all the grandparents moved there. These were the years before the boom, when it was largely a senior's retirement town, and an affordable middle-class settler vacation spot. We'd stay in low-budget motels with outdoor pools. Spend our days at the waterslide park or the Scandia Golf & Games playing minigolf or Skee-Ball. Bedrock City was a favourite haunt, the Flintstones-themed amusement park that was a yabba-dabba "gay" old time. (The whole city more or less frozen since the '60s.) But we spent most of our time at the small, family-oriented beach south of the bridge, a more secluded and quiet spot than the larger Boyce-Gyro Beach Park.

The Kelowna of our childhood, of course, is no more. Gentrified and expensive, it's now the summer home of hockey players and rich people.

The night before I have to do the thing I don't want to have to do, my body and mind wage a full-on revolt. I start screaming without making a sound. Jonathon and I have camped out in our friends Darren and Sue's basement, where we've set our cats up with litter, food and water. When we let them out of their carriers, they carefully sniff every inch of carpet.

The meltdown starts on Facebook. I don't remember the trigger. I'm self-immolating and can't control my emotions or actions. I don't remember what I say, but I remove my profile picture and delete my account. Shoes, sweater. Leave the house without thinking and walk. My heart is pounding and I can't slow it down. I get to a field and wind my way around the perimeter, avoiding a youth baseball game. The field is flanked by CP Rail tracks and a running path. I sit on a bench with my pounding heart and feel detached as I watch cyclists and dog-walkers pass. They belong to the world of the living, and it's not my world anymore. My face is hot and I can't breathe.

Behind me, a willow tree's long leaves sway in the hot breeze.

I can't tell if I'm waiting to muster the courage to stand on the tracks, or waiting to muster the courage to get up and go back to Darren and Sue's. Either way, I'm fucked. Hamlet's soliloquy makes sense for the first time in my life. I need to delay tomorrow; I'm not strong enough to do it. I can't do it.

Chris, I can't do it.

The Tallest Man on Earth comes to Mac Hall Ballroom in Calgary. I wait around until the very end when all the ticket holders have left, the crew is tearing down and security is nowhere in sight. Then I bust into Kristian Matsson's dressing room with the fire of a thousand suns. I know that my behaviour is unhinged and possibly assaultive, but this is what I do for the first two years after your death: Seek out the most tenuous connections to you. Look for you everywhere. Ask random people, "Did you know him, did you know him, did you know him?"

Matsson is standing shirtless, jeans, no socks, a bearded backup musician puttering beside him. The Tallest Man on Earth is actually not that tall – he's short, fine-boned and pretty in that slightly clichéd unkempt artist's way.

He looks at beardo – "Do you know . . . ?"

"No one knows me." I take a breath.

Chris, I'd been calm and clear when interviewed by the media about your death. I kept my composure when I spoke at your funeral. I was eloquent and clear when Marc asked me to speak impromptu at his art show for you. But standing in front of this shirtless stranger whose song has charted my path, my mouth floods. I feel my face contort into an ugly cry. I can barely form words between the sobs.

I tell him about you, and that his music has been important in my grief. I tell him that one song in particular kept me alive. I tell him my brother was a musician, too, Chris from Women, maybe you met him? I know your bands shared a European booking agent.

He nods, says quietly, "I knew him. I'm sorry."

Then he closes the space between us and wraps his arms around me. My tears drip onto his naked shoulder, his skin warm under my cheek. And I'm in Okanagan Lake with the silt of your body floating out of my hands; I'm in the back seat of the minivan beside you flipping picture books; I'm at the crematorium holding hands with our family, watching your plywood box slide into the fire; I'm in a dressing room hugging a stranger.

*

I haven't been to our beach in a decade or more. We have to use a map to find it. Jonathon parks the U-Haul a block and a half away. I go alone, a screwdriver in the left thigh pocket of my cargo pants, the little pedal box in my right. My hands are shaking.

I make my way slowly down the street, evil in my pocket. Broken shards where a man used to be. There's the lake, the beach, the park and the sprawling grounds of the Kelowna General Hospital beyond. There used to be more park and less hospital, if I remember correctly. It got annexed over the years. Baba would come here when she was suffering from heart pain and palpitations, before her angioplasty. Mom and I had a screaming match in the parking lot circa 1996 when they were trying to teach me how to park the minivan and I couldn't get it right.

An elderly gentleman, a cancer patient judging from his bald head and grey pallor, sits on a bench at the edge of the park, with a son or a nephew. The younger man looks right at me, his eyes bore into mine and I feel that he knows the illegal act I am about to commit. I walk midway down the beach and kneel in the sand. Chris, is this your will or mine?

I carefully unscrew the bottom of the metal box and stuff the screws into my pocket. It was Marc's idea to use the same small boxes you'd been using to make guitar effects pedals for our individual mini urns. The baggie is closed with a zip tie, which I saw off with a pocket knife.

A black beetle alights on the back of my hand.

I leave the box and my shoes on the sand and walk toward the water.

Families are formed in a hundred different ways but often built in reverse. We know who we are through the stories we're told and the familiar faded pictures on walls. Here I am as a child on my birthday. Here's Dido in a suit and tie, smiling in front of someone's liquor cabinet. Here's Baba and Dido in a Kodachrome colour photo on their wedding day. Look how the crease in all our foreheads is the same. See these dead ancestors in their fur coats, short and pudgy against the weathered prairie.

Nostalgia is a dangerous emotion, leading easily to crass sentimentality. After your death, I take up residence there.

Ashes, for the uninitiated, are not the ashes of a cigarette but shards and fragments of bone. The skin and the organs are burned away in the fire, leaving the skeleton, which is pulverized and ground up in a machine called a cremulator. The resultant material is not unlike a rocky sand.

I walk into the lake up to my knees and crouch down. I have a portion of all that is left of your material life, and I scoop it into my palm then let it go into the water, warm and clear and clean. This is your baptism in reverse. Your dust falls away from my outstretched fingers and floats into the lake.

Something in my body lets go.

It feels right to leave this part of you here, to give you back to the current of our childhood. You belong to this lake like you have always belonged to this lake, blond hair bleaching and skin browning in your swimming trunks, bobbing on our inflatable boat for hours. Your skin and muscles and heart and bone belong here with sand and rocks and rainbow trout.

It's only when I get back to my shoes that I notice the beetle is still with me. I watch it for a while, little metallic body and sticky feet clinging to my pale hand speckled with water droplets. It remains there as I fumble to close the baggie and what's left of your dust inside the pedal box, then it raises its wings and flies away.

FOUR:
CLINICAL ZONES

THE ROYAL JUBILEE HOSPITAL, VICTORIA

Richard Harrison

I'm at home now, twenty-two days after my mother chose to die with the help of a physician rather than linger in what some call "a battle against cancer." In her case, the lymphoma would have killed her in three months, six tops, after an unbearably long period of losses and pain, and for what? So we could say she fought? There would have been no fight, only the morality play we make people go through so we can comfort ourselves with the idea that of all things, we value life the most. Or rather, probably less politically said, so we can comfort ourselves with the thought that the dying would do anything rather than leave us when clearly that is not the truth.

I'm surrounded by the paper connections Mum had with Canadian society – her pension notices, cable bills, bank accounts, income tax forms – because even though she's dead, Mum still owes and is owed. These are the pages that knock on doors. Every one of them is some link between my mother and strangers who've been good to her, lived up to their bargains without ever knowing, most of them, who she was. But it's been a while since I wrote anything for its own sake, just for words, content to be the words they are in the stillness of the mind. This is one of those times when I remember why so many young poets (and I mean young in the sense that no matter their age, they are just beginning to take that poetic sensibility from its silence and writing with it) start with lost love: lost love sits you right down the way death does and says, "Don't move." And I am still, and still not sure what I'm writing: a letter, a free-written draft of a poem; an essay about grief because grief is here now, just down the road from the room where Mum died. But even if I don't know what I'm writing, I know I'm writing because I'm writing to you.

I remember reading "Shall I compare thee to a Summer's day?" with my poetry group; the conclusion of our discussion was that Shakespeare wasn't writing to a specific lover but to the reader, whoever and whenever they were. The guarantee in the poem, that the person written to would outlast its moment, wasn't an exaggeration; it was the truth about how readers keep poems awake, how readers keep writing alive.

Time went strangely. In the days leading up to the day, even while talking to my wife, Lisa, on the phone, I would check the time, forget it within minutes, and need to check it again. It's a weird feeling, in the oldest sense of that word, to forget the meaning of time. My brother Tony and I were in the room with Mum for about two hours before the doctor arrived, and I can't remember how those two hours were spent. We talked, we had visitors – the nurses loved her and they came to say goodbye and embrace her and she drank it all in. I've never seen my mother happier for longer than in the last ten days of her life. And of course, it was the stuff of theatre that made it possible – a clear schedule of what would happen when, a rotating cast of health care workers, or intermittent visits by those who were there from the start. And Tony and I there every afternoon, taking in the stories, paying attention, loving all the same things, because at that point there was nothing else to do. Even then we made a few missteps; for at least four days, Mum was distressed that neither of us liked *Lady Cottington's Pressed Fairy Book*, which Mum had back in her apartment and nicknamed *The Squashed Fairy Book*, which looks exactly the way the nickname makes it sound. But even that disagreement was essential in its way – no one believes you if you always agree with them.

And you know, we did learn, we learned, and my brother and I put aside the old causes of our rivalry and fear of each other. That is the gift we gave each other as part of what we made for us all, the creation at the end of her life of the family that Mum wanted us to have always been; we created the brotherly relationship the family had kept wounded. I am going through the survivor's anger at the dead and I know it. Somewhere the poem out of all this is a lament for the mother I got a glimpse of in those last ten days, the one who ate ice cream for the first time in over thirty years because she wasn't concerned anymore about her health or the weight of her thin, tiny body.

No more meals of brown rice and a sliver of cheese or fish – the full filets on her tray turned the hospital food into the kind of board for which a gourmet groans; she delighted in the rotation of tilapia, macaroni and cheese, and chicken Alfredo, and then delighted in it all over. She put on weight, gained strength; by the end, she was able to push her own walker up the path to the centre of the garden she went to every day with us to sit and feed sunflower seeds to the sparrows, and Cheezies to the one crow that liked them. In the end, she was bigger and stronger and happier than I'd seen her in years, and this I've already said, but I need to circle back the way the story did. . . . She had ice cream and Gouda cheese for her last breakfast. She loved it in a way she never let herself love food in all the time I knew her.

Here's something I just remembered: somewhere in those last two hours that seemed past before they were even present, Mum took a moment to tell me that on the second shelf of the linen closet in the second bedroom, the one unused since Dad went into the Lodge thirteen years ago, there was a bag with some protective underwear, but that the bag had never been opened, and that even though there was no receipt, I could take it back to Shoppers and get her money back. Even when we think we've let go of everything, to our own selves we are true, and she was always the most prudent of consumers.

But this time, she let her pride out. She was proud of her accomplishments. She was proud of us. She was proud of her grandchildren. And she told everyone – and everyone told us what a great lady she was, and that she had found the perfect moment to be the very best she could be. She read poems, and I wondered where the voice of poetry that had been with her all her life had been hiding. But I know the answer to that, and if I didn't tell the truth of my mother's life, there would be nothing to learn from it. The truth is, her poetry was swallowed up in the lifetime of argument she had with my father, a man she stayed bound to all her life – and kept him bound to her – by the rules of the culture that raised her and exists today the way a broken vase exists in a box in the basement because no one can fix it or bring themselves to throw it out.

My mother loved the poems "Ducks," "Miss Thompson Goes Shopping" and "Nicholas Nye," poems she'd studied in school in England and poems I'd never heard of until she mentioned them once, years ago, and had me find copies to send to her. I found them in her apartment in the original envelope I'd sent them in and brought them on a visit, and she read them into my cell phone, some bits by heart. She'd recited some A. A. Milne to us when we were very young, and the songs from *The Wind in the Willows*, but the poetry stopped for her when it was clear that the poetry my dad was reciting, and the connections it made between him and my brother and me, were connections she didn't have. So she withdrew, partly because we were men and no matter how my mother loved her sons, men were never unthreatening to her.

She said goodbye to the world with Tony and me reading her alternate verses of "Ode to a Nightingale." Her favourite line in it: "half in love with easeful Death." And she was, I see that now, she was always half in love with the end of pain and sorrow. She didn't so much hold on to the pain of the War as she became someone different after it, a person who never found her way back to who she was before it all began and never gave up mourning her loss. Her war story, though it started, of course, with the Nazis, had little to do with them. For her it was That Man and what he had done, That Man to whose home in the countryside she was sent to save her, as it was meant to save thousands of children, from the War, That Man with his cock extended toward her in the night, in the meagre light the blackout curtains held in, a pale cock she never touched, she was always insistent on that, but the image of which she never released. And that, too, is the result of her time and how it failed women and children. My mother died one of millions. And I think she also somehow began dreaming of the end of all sorrow then, of that easeful Death that she could love, and in the end, he came for her and she was serene.

Death came in the form of a kind doctor, a woman my mother liked, and her kit of syringes. Even she, the doctor who'd performed medically assisted deaths many times, was impressed with how clear Mum was in wanting it. And I don't know that we ever look right into someone's soul or mind or even desire, but if we can, then I say I saw my mother in love at last when she held our hands and looked into that doctor's kind and steady eyes, and the drugs moved through their intimacy with the vein in her arm and let her slide into sleep (still talking about her sons) and then into incoherence, and then soft snores, and then silence to us, and then silence to the stethoscope.

I wept. I'd done as she asked and not cried while the injections were going in one after the other and she was fading, but afterwards I couldn't help it. And Tony, who had cried in the hall when we were ushered out to give her the second last chance she'd have to say no to dying at 10:15 that morning, to the doctor with her boxes of syringes marked "MAiD," he comforted me with a hand on my shoulder. And the whole time, Henry, the stuffed toy dragon, who my daughter Emma made for her, was perched on Mum's collarbone. Everyone admired Henry, and Mum said of him, "Look at his eyes, begging, 'Love me!'"

We held Mum's hands for a while, then we cleaned up the room because that's the way Mum was with rooms and that felt okay. And we touched her arm and her cheek over the next hour, and her body became cool, and her fingers purple with the blood in them that was stranded there and dying, too. The nurse said that three hours was the limit of how long we could stay, and I said, "I've seen the changes," and she said, "There are more," and I knew I didn't want to see them. I kissed my Mum on the forehead because that was the part of her least changed by death. And Henry rubbed his face on her cheek because I had said goodbye as a man but not a child.

SCATTERED

Catherine Greenwood

When my father died in the Alzheimer's ward of Victoria's Gorge Road Hospital in the autumn of 2015, just ten days short of his eighty-fifth birthday, we were both in a state of displacement. My husband was working in England, and after a summer of renovations I was in the middle of final negotiations for selling our home, for though we loved its light-filled rooms and had been happy there, it was time to let it go. On a Thursday afternoon at work, I was waiting for the results of the buyer's house inspection when I got a call from the Gorge regarding my father's condition. His heart rate, the nurse said, was erratic, and she wanted to confirm that the family didn't wish to subject him to the stress of being transported to Emergency. Are you saying he's dying? I asked. Well, sometimes they hang on for a week or two, she said. I took that as a yes and shut down my computer.

A year earlier I'd booked a day off to see Jimmy settled into the Arbutus wing when he was moved there from the general hospital where he'd been recovering from yet another urinary tract infection. Suffering from bladder cancer and dementia at the same time, his deteriorating health made it impossible for my mother to continue caring for him at home. After unpacking his few belongings and getting him acquainted with his corner of a room shared with three other old and unwell men, I made a break for it, waving brightly from the end of the corridor to where he peered anxiously after me, hastily buckling his belt over his housecoat, hoping to be taken home. Thus incarcerated, his decline was hastened by a lack of physiotherapy and an over-application of tranquilizers. On one occasion I arrived to find him fully dressed and on his knees beside his bed, doing a face plant on the mattress. I'd roamed the ward seeking help, and an orderly who looked like he might practise mixed martial arts in his spare time came and righted him, but not without a tussle. It's okay, Jim, I'm your friend, he said, gripping my father's fists in his own as gently as he could. He asked me if Dad had been a boxer. He has some moves, said the guy, approvingly.

The night my father died was bedlam. Herb's TV was blaring at full volume, the other Jim, the tall one, had fallen out of his bed opposite Dad's and was crawling across the floor in his diaper, and a woman holding a plastic baby was blocking the door with her wheelchair and yelling. My father lay blinking beneath the glare of the fluorescent lights, an oxygen tube in his nose and a single tear slipping down his cheek.

Finally, after the chaos of the bedtime rush, a nurse was available to supervise Jimmy's last move to a private room with a dimmer switch. I rehung his calendar and his Castle Cary pipe band T-shirt on the cinder-block walls and placed the photos of his grandchildren on the bedside table. The nurse left me with a paper cup full of ice chips and mint-flavoured mouth swabs. When she checked in an hour later, she noted the spreading skein of blood vessels on his face and the long rasping breaths, and asked if it was important for my mother to be there when he passed. I'd written numerous letters to hospital administrators in a failed attempt to have Dad moved to a facility nearer to my mother, Anne, who lived over an hour's drive away. By the time she arrived by taxi that night, his final pulse had been taken and his limbs straightened. He looked like a plant gone to seed, his mottled head a spent and shrivelled pod. After the doctor signed the death certificate, we left him there, hesitantly and somewhat in shock, cleaving to the promise that someone called Bob from Earth's Options was coming to collect and cremate his remains.

This could not have been the end Jimmy imagined when he immigrated to Canada from Scotland. Born in Glasgow, he sometimes holidayed with his aunt on the Shetland Islands, where as a young sailor on leave from the merchant navy he met my mother over a game of badminton. They married in 1956 and moved to Vancouver Island, where they spent most of their lives, except for a brief stint ranching in BC's Boundary district. His mother and younger siblings eventually followed him to the island. When my grandmother died at age ninety-six in a Crofton care home, she also held a subscription to a cremation service. My father took custody of the cardboard box of ashes and commissioned a memorial plaque, a plum granite slab inscribed with Gran's vital statistics and the unquestioned assertion that she had been Loved by All Who Knew Her.

His suitcase must have tipped the scales at the airport. Without so much as a death certificate to verify its contents, he flew off to Shetland to stay with my mother's nephew, who, through local connections, helped Dad bypass any regulatory obstacles to him planting his mother's cremains in a corner of her own family's plot, beside her sister and parents. A memorial service had, of course, been held for Gran's family on Vancouver Island, but my Shetland cousin was bestowed with the power of a local religious affiliation, and after helping Dad dig the hole and cement the granite marker in place, read out appropriate words from his Bible. Back in Canada, we were shown photos of this interment. I'm not sure who of Gran's five children and their offspring, beside my parents and myself, has attended her final resting place. Shetland is a long way away.

Without planning to, our family continued this tradition, a diaspora of ash. Six weeks after Dad's death we reconvened in Victoria, my two brothers and their families coming from Winnipeg and Quesnel for a memorial gathering. My husband had returned from England for the occasion and we were paying winter rates to stay in a roadside motel. At that point my life was a series of small suitcases and black plastic garbage bags full of clothes. (During this period, I had become the Bearer of Bad Tidings, informing my husband in England by Skype of our beloved cat's death and our electrical system's lack of a permit; my mother as she anxiously entered the nursing home's dim corridor of her husband's death just minutes earlier; my employer of my need to take a short-term stress leave; and, upon my return to work, my overburdened co-worker of my decision to quit in a month's time. I spoke, people cried or at the least looked horribly dismayed. I had yet to advise my family of complications around the will.) After a spate of errands related to executing my father's estate, I was relieved to again unpack my suitcase and settle in to the dingy, dust-mote quietude of the motor court for a week, leaving the organization of the memorial service to my brothers while Steve and I attended to our own affairs.

The day after the memorial service, on a dry November Sunday, the family gathered around a new pear tree decanted into a freshly dug hole and took turns dipping a flour scoop into the plastic bag of cremains, sprinkling the powder over the root ball, along with whatever words we each summoned and directed down into the black soil. Bone meal, something to make Dad's long-desired pear tree grow among the small orchard of apples he'd cultivated and cared for over the past quarter-century. My brother Jason, the gardener, filled in the hole with a shovel and steadied the tree with two stakes. There's a photo, possibly the last that will ever be taken of our entire family together – siblings, spouses and children in a semicircle around the tree, and at the centre of this grouping my mother, a thin grey twig, supported by a son and son-in-law on either side.

Before I closed the box of ashes, Mom took a final scoop from the plastic bag inside and whisked around, anointing unmarked spots in the yard, somewhere near the base of a fir tree and the side of the garage, naming with each toss of grey grit the pets buried there as she liberally salted the earth with Dad's ashes: Barrack, the shy Saluki-cross; Evinrude, the ginger tom with the loud motor; Smidgeon, the tiny tabby who'd outlived them all; and Cappy, Dad's border collie (for whose loss he'd wept harder than he had for anyone, even his mother. This I now understood – Prudence, our sixteen-year-old calico cat, presiding spirit of our household, had died three weeks prior to my father. The vet came to the house and administered the shots, and I watched as her sleep shifted into a vacancy that prepared me for the moment I'd find myself sitting alone beside my father's untenanted body. I have never wailed as long and as loudly as I did for my pestering, gorgeous, stubborn and unforgettable familiar. Her death was kinder than my father's and her ashes packaged in a more-seemly bamboo box, and when the house sold a few days later, my friend Deborah and I tossed them with a plastic spoon over Prudence's sunny place in the backyard, where they lay on the grass like lines on a playing field).

I left the country a month after Dad's memorial, unmoored from my old life, with a freshly sutured hole in my head from a root canal gone wrong, carrying Prudence's clay paw print and fur swatch (a cardboard-backed sample of black, orange and ivory fibres with which I can mentally summon a cat-golem but that also resembles the shedding fake-fur with which I tried to stitch a stuffed cat in a junior high crafts class). Sometime that winter the pear tree, which Mom had named Jimmy, died unexpectedly, snapping at the base of the trunk and devastating her all over again. I promised that we would plant a new one when I came to visit in the spring.

We went to Canadian Tire and got a smaller pear tree, one that fit into the back of the station wagon. Dad's ashes, in increments, now resided in a shortbread canister with a purple thistle on a red tartan background. On the evening of what would have been their sixtieth wedding anniversary, Mom and I took the tin to nearby Taylor Beach, one of their favourite places to walk the dog. I found a stick and scratched Jimmy's name into a smooth patch of sand, and Anne opened the tin to set him free upon the hushed retreating waves, along with a single red rose.

That was the first of three scatterings that year. That summer, Mom flew to England to visit us, and Steve and I accompanied her north to Shetland. With her sole surviving brother, we visited the kirkyard where Dad had taken his mother. A bitterly windy day, the saturated green splendour of grass and stone, a choppy grey ocean in the near distance; Anne and David, arm in arm, seeking amid rows of white granite the bones of their parents and brothers. We laid bunches of pink and yellow carnations on their graves, and against a headstone pitched over a patch of empty earth, placeholder for the youngest and brightest brother lost at sea. When we found Dad's family plot, wind and dirt had all but erased the inscription from his mother's plaque. I read aloud a few words from the only book I had brought with me, Heaney's translation of *Beowulf*, Shield's funeral:

> They stretched out their beloved lord in his boat,
> laid out by the mast, amidships,
> the great ring-giver. Far-fetched treasures
> were piled upon him, and precious gear.

Not exactly accurate, but apt enough. My father, known as the Wee Man, had been the eldest of his siblings, and they had followed him to Canada, one by one. Now we were back here, where the gale nearly knocked over my mother, suddenly kneecapped by grief. Steve wrenched the lid from the tartan tin and we took turns sprinkling the ashes, heavier in the wind than one might expect, in a thin line around Gran's stone.

That autumn I visited Canada again and took my mother to the High Croft ranch in BC's Boundary district. In a Lear-like act of folly, at the onset of his dementia, he had signed the property over to the older of my two brothers – a transaction conducted in secrecy and discovered after it was no longer fair or feasible to confront him. Out came the tin again, refilled like a Celtic pot of plenty. Mom wanted me to drive to the top of the mountain, so we could scatter him where he'd always wanted to build a circular house with windows open to the panoramic views. I wouldn't risk the car's undercarriage on the rocky overgrown track, and Mom couldn't walk that far, so she settled for shaking the tin's contents over the red Hesston mower abandoned by the barn.

It has been generally assumed, in our family, that Dad would want his ashes scattered at the ranch. But I wonder: Why not Glasgow, where he was born? Or Japan, where he went often in later life, to study the language and to be with friends he'd made? He was raised Protestant but was not a churchgoer, and was interested in Buddhism in the last decades of his life. I think of our trip to Japan, and a perfect, peaceful sunny day together on Miyajima Island. We often disagreed, and there was a struggle between us that never ended, though it was eventually abandoned. But that afternoon, the tide was out and we walked across the mud flat to the famous Torii gates, and touched its huge timbers painted with creosote while Anne waited on shore, waving and fending off the deer as she tried to eat a granola bar. Dad beamed that day, sharing this magical place with us.

That's where I scatter him now, whether or not there are ashes left to fill the tin.

After Dad's death, there was no time for grief. I'd spent it all on the cat and was a walking husk, a papier mâché of documents animated by electronic signatures and sustained by white wine. Once the doctor had been summoned to come and sign the death certificate, long after midnight, I drove my mother home from the Gorge Hospital and picked my brother Jason up at the airport the next morning. That day I started composing an obituary and finalized the deal on our house. I had two weeks to vacate, and with the help of friends I packed and sold what furnishings remained after staging the place, an elegant set upon which would-be buyers could imagine the drama of their lives unfolding. It was as if I had been living for the last few weeks in someone else's dream.

One afternoon, I noticed an elderly woman standing on the sidewalk and pointing out the property to her companion. I wondered if it was the large green storage container sitting in the driveway that caught her attention, or if she was the mother of the new owner. But the object of her gaze was a large snapdragon that had seeded itself in the gravel verge, a deep magenta volunteer. My father's favourite colour was cerise, the colour of a crinkly foil candy wrapper he remembered from a rare childhood holiday at the seaside. I took a closer look when I next went outside and saw two creamy blossoms on one side of the stalk as if grafted there, puffy as a pair of boxing gloves. It was a message from my father, in the pink and punching above his weight.

As for the pear tree, this new Jimmy has rooted and survives, and, in a weird act of cannibalism, took Anne's wedding ring when she was watering him. The neighbour came over with a metal detector but couldn't find it. That's okay, Mom said, when she told me over the phone. We're here together now.

THRALL: A YEAR OF GRIEVING

Catherine Owen

This is the land where I became a widow. Edmonton, Alberta. I am back a year after his death on April 11th, 2010, to perform at the Edmonton Poetry Festival. His death. Him. My spouse of eight years, Christopher George Matzigkeit, twenty-nine years old, 5'11", 140 or so pounds, brown, somewhat scraggly hair, greeny eyes – is that what colour they were? I seem to already be forgetting, though I know there was a pebbled notch of a scar in his forehead, he could never grow a full beard and he bore a tattoo that said "Live for the Pit" below his squinchy navel, across his smooth, ridged abdomen. His death.

I have never felt so ambivalent about a place as I do now toward Edmonton. Its dust, magpies, snow. Its incredible wealths and poverties. We lived here, Chris and I, for three and a half years, from 2006 to 2009. During that time, we constructed a dream; we dismantled it. At our peak, he worked hard boilermaking, I writing, and we afforded instruments, a home recording studio, mini-tours and gigs with our metal bands, Inhuman and Helgrind. We cared for a dog, several cats, houseplants. We composed together, devoured overflowing bowls of cereal while watching episodes of *Dexter*, hosted a performance series, walked by the North Saskatchewan River holding hands. There is no satisfactory way to sum up any long-term relationship. And once it's over, what could be harder than trying to recall the day in, day out complexity of the shared compact: the glue, the nuances, the absurdities. The writer Joyce Carol Oates, even after being married to her husband, Ray, for forty-seven years, achingly acknowledges in her memoir that "what is frightening is, maybe . . . [i]n some essential way, I never knew my husband." Even after such an extensive period of connubial togetherness, a bond that shaped nearly every decision and act from the time she was twenty-two, Joyce wonders whether, now that Ray is suddenly dead, their bond truly mattered, if in the larger scheme of things her union with a now-deceased person had any meaning at all.

Ray died at seventy-seven, from pneumonia's complications, a death Oates still interprets as unjust, premature. As it always is, regardless of facts – this harsh, permanent, removal of a loved one. Chris died at twenty-nine. From a heart attack. Due to an erratic, intermittent yet horrifically final addiction to crack, an addiction that had followed in the smoke of other habits, including a reliance on alcohol, cigarettes, weed and, prior to our relationship, several years spent hooked on acid. Was this death unjust, premature, too? Or had his actions, as one might bluntly assess, brought his death upon himself? Was his death, in fact, merciful when placed alongside the likelihood of continued erosion? Nine weeks of crack addiction, separated by two years of being clean. Nine weeks in which his already slender figure plunged to emaciation, any level of hygiene vanished. He seemed to be alternately hyperactive, existing in a delusional space of superhumanness, minus any obvious accomplishments, and sluggish, constantly sleeping, restlessly, tooth-grindingly, sniffingly, hoodie yanked low over his ears, eyes, cheekbones hard hafts beneath. Nine weeks in which he pawned many of his beloved instruments, a video camera, his second leather jacket once so carefully painted with Odin's hammer on the back. Nine weeks of writing thousands of dollars of bad cheques and concocting preposterous and dangerous ideas for everything from holding up banks to running porn companies, all in order to make a quick buck, money readily translatable to one of those white rocks, cooked up with baking soda, tamped with steel wool, sucked up through a glass pipe. The high lasts minutes, sometimes less. The hunger never leaves. Nine weeks of which I witnessed only ten or twelve days.

He had first become addicted when I was in Europe for five weeks in 2007. After I returned and finally grew aware of his addiction, he got clean in a matter of days, superficially and far too cockily as I later realized. During the two years between his active usage, I took care of the cash flow and, as much as possible, his health, and we tried to rebuild what was left of our life in this land. Then, I went on a book tour in fall 2009. Within three days (despite so many promises) he was addicted again. I returned in five weeks to no home, many of the animals gone, he back at his parents' place in the interior of BC and me needing to dispose of the possessions that remained fast, before departing for my own parents' place in Vancouver. Once he'd been clean again for several months, we began (almost unbelievably!) to imagine yet another type of future together, however much friends and family were opposed to our reuniting. We had split from each other, but the missing had been too immense. And yet, then, what did I know of missing? We met three more times for weekends in Kamloops, Vancouver and, in the end, Edmonton, where, feeling dangerously immune to addiction once more, Chris had obtained work and was living in a small, leaky trailer. When I was with him though, we stayed in hotels. There was giddy, ridiculous hope. Eating pizza, shopping at Value Village, composing a new song, even the one terrible fight we had, all reassured us that a trip back to some form of normalcy as a couple was possible.

Apart, we spoke on the phone up to five times a day. I watched documentaries on addiction; he read books on communication. Hope, hope. Too much hope. After Chris died, my father said to me, sitting at the side of my bed, patting my hand with calloused, rhythmic tenderness, "It must have been as if he was crossing the street toward you, beaming, arms held out in anticipated embrace when, from nowhere, a truck wiped him out; right in front of you, he was gone." Yes, that is what it was like. After I found out Chris was dead, I didn't know what was, or would have been, worse. If he had died without us reconciling, distanced by my maybe-sane refusal to accept his premature version of our fantasized future, knowing by then how very low the chances are of a crack addict coming permanently clean. Or dying as he did, after I had begun to feel for him again, after we had forgiven each other for the pain we had caused, pledged a life as one, begun writing music together once more; after the last words he had said to me were "I love you, baby, I've never felt closer to you." Of course, the latter. In that choice to continue to believe, even irrationally, foolishly, even if the pain now is worse because of this, I have no regrets.

The Call, April 11th, 2010

Sitting eating brunch on Whyte Avenue at the Artisan Resto-Cafe a few days into the festival, I am struck by the sight of a young blond boy, about three or four years old, sharing a meal with his likely exhausted and thus subtly vacant mother. The boy looks around him restlessly, then turns and stares at me like a pure beam of light, his smile wholly open. His small teeth glow in my direction and I am forced to look away. I cannot bear such transparencies anymore. In this instant, I am reminded of photos I saw of Chris as a child, the wheat and gentle honey of him. What will become of you, is all I can think as this boy looks at me. How much will you eventually lose?

The ineptitude with which we often deal with death, even from those supposedly in charge of its follow-up procedures, is only matched in horror by the equal prevalence of the curt, inappropriate efficiency certain institutions offer the griever. Hours after not receiving my morning call from Chris, and he then not picking up when I phoned, I knew immediately he was either back on crack or dead. "He probably just forgot his phone somewhere," my mother suggested. "Maybe he got called into work unexpectedly," others tried. No. I knew he was gone, though as it was too early to report him missing, I had no choice but to continue to dial his number every fifteen minutes, all day, all night, in between desperately trying to keep busy by working on a collage of us I was calling *The Bond*, a canvas that featured cut-up photos of our body parts, including a close-up of our hands clasped together, and beneath, the new tattoo on his forearm he'd had inked for his twenty-ninth birthday six weeks earlier: the word "Endurance." The tension between my internal knowledge and the need to follow external protocol was unbearable. Why did I have to wait twenty-four hours to report him missing when I knew right away that things had gone desperately wrong?

The next day, early, after a sleepless night of continuing to call his phone until it ran out of batteries, repeating the mantra, "The customer you are dialing is currently out of the service area," I phoned the Gibbons police department to fill out a missing person report. They thanked me for the information, said they would refer it to the Edmonton detachment as well and get back to me with any news. I waited. I waited some more. Surely they would call. "They'll call if they find him," my mother reassured me. How we want to believe in the essential goodwill of authority figures. So, I waited. Hours later, exasperated, needing to assert some sense of control, I called back. "Just a moment," the person who answered said, and then a rough-voiced man, the sergeant at the Gibbons station, got on the phone. "Oh, yes," he replied, not even asking me to sit down first, not even saying he was sorry, terribly sorry but he had awful news for me, "there was a body found matching your description. It was located in downtown Edmonton, Jasper Avenue. Yes, in a silver Dodge Dakota. No, I have no further information. You'll have to call the coroner for that. Do you want his number?"

In a daze, I took the numerals down. Why were there no officers at my door summoned by the Edmonton detachment to deliver this terrifying tale in person, to offer me Kleenexes, to pat my shoulder? How was I possibly hearing this horror story, in brief, over the cold phone? Then I called the coroner and was met by an unimaginable chill. "Yes," he gruffed out, "there's a body here. You'll have to get down to identify it." "I'm in Vancouver," I stammered, "I'll try to fly there today." "If you don't get here by this afternoon," he said, issuing an ultimatum, "I'll have to get one of his other contacts to identify him." "No! I'm his spouse. I'll be there as soon as I can." "Well I'm just letting you know you better be. You need directions?" "Yes, I'll be there!" I emphasized, trembling. "Just don't let anyone else identify him!" I dropped the phone, let my brother and mother know that a "body bearing my description had been found in a truck downtown" – awful words that continue to haunt me with their sickening anonymity – and let them begin to take care of the initial business to be accomplished: booking the flight.

The Viewing, April 12th, 2010

I am here again, in Edmonton, for the Poetry Festival at nearly the same time of year I was arriving for the viewing last April, supported by my brother on one side, a man whose legalistic eloquence would become such an unsuspected boon during the form-filled days ahead as he navigated the crevices that Chris and I, with our tenuous common-law relationship, fell between, making the retrieval of his truck and personal effects from the police impound challenging, even compromising my ability to obtain his autopsy report as we were not living at the same address when he died. And, on the other side, by my mother's gentle sopping up of my relentless tears, her reminding me to eat, breathe. The snow was at a similar stage of erasure: soiled spines of ice still limning every roadway, groggy grasses uncrumpling, a sky so shiftless above and above and above us.

Fortunately, I was not met in the foyer by the coroner, that insensate, disembodied voice, but by Calvin, a black man wearing scarlet and smelling of cinnamon – a professional comforter by trade who, after I filled out the first of what would be many, many forms, led me down one hall then another as I asked him flailing questions that he somehow folded and handed softly back to me as answers, however partial: "How did he die? Do we know?" "Seems like his heart gave out, dear." "But why?" "That we aren't sure of. They did toxicology tests but it will take three or four months to come back with any results." "Drugs? Could it have been an overdose?" "Quite possibly. Did he have problems with that? There was an open bottle of something found on the seat beside him. Or it may have been natural." "At twenty-nine?" "Oh, these things happen at any age, miss."

Calvin eventually led me into a dimmed room, brown carpet, furnished only by one chair, the far wall hung with a heavy drape. "Now," he intoned slowly, "I'm going to open this curtain from the far end to the near one, and when you can see it's him, you let me know, dear."

Nothing had prepared me for this procedure. In the crime dramas I had watched, bodies at the morgue were always pulled unceremoniously from steel drawers like cumbersome cutlery, toe-tagged, sheet yanked quickly off the face for identification. Not this endless mechanical whirring back of a curtain to reveal a wrapped-in-blue dummy shape. Throughout the entire painstaking and overly dramatic unveiling I was trying to convince myself it could not be him. Would he ever be clad in a cornflower sheet like an insipid saint? Of course not! And then, unbearably, it was him. The curtain had stopped moving, had reached the far wall and there was his face. His face! (I cried out.) Then I screamed, "It's him, it's him!" Though "him" was only a bared head now, horribly deific in the cooler room behind a pane of thick glass, suited absurdly in that crimped, crisp institutional halo of cotton, his perfect face shaved, cheekbones hard, frozen, the only sign of the violence of his end a contusion on his lower lip where he had likely bitten down fast as his heart was hit by that clot, as it burst.

Calvin handed me a Kleenex like a rose. "How long were you together?" he asked quietly. "Eight years." "Oh, a long time, a long time. It'll be hard. Anything you need you just let me know. Should I leave you alone for a minute?" "Yes, yes. Can I take pictures?" "Of course, anything you need." And so, I snapped one, two shots. I wanted to show others, look, here's proof, he's dead, it's really him, and when I showed my mother she would exclaim, "The sweetheart, oh!" I talked to Chris behind the pane, within his shroud for a while, asking him how, when, why, all those awful and pointless questions, those wholly unanswerable pleas, weeping. And then Calvin took me by the arm, gentle suitor of death, and led me back to the foyer. "Have you thought of a funeral home?" "No!" "Well here's a card for Simply Cremations. Many of our clients have used their services before and been satisfied." "Oh. Okay." "You make arrangements, dear, and then the body . . . Chris . . . will be transported there later on today, all right? You be sure to let us know." "I will." "Good. It was nice to meet you, miss. And I wish it could have been under better circumstances." As he left me with my mother and brother, I stared after him, his stately, slippered walk through the hush of the morgue, and wondered what those might have been.

Simply Cremations, April 13th, 2010

Calvin. I haven't forgotten him. Nor will I forget the waiter who, not knowing that I am so struck by grief on this morning, a year later, that I can barely glance at the loving couple opposite me with their awkward, adoring grins and nervous finger touches over mugs of hot coffee, serves me my eggs Benny with such a lovely flourish, exclaiming, "Here you are, my dearest!" Grief has obliterated much, but it has also lifted the kindnesses of acquaintances and even total strangers into the light, making me incapable of taking for granted these little gifts of gesture, tone, those holy, gracious moments.

Widows say the craziest things. Oates, upon seeing Ray's body, newly chill, in the hospital room bed, gasped out, "Oh, honey, what has happened to you!" her voice rising, as if by the increased volume she would rouse him from this strange slumber. I, too, upon looking at Chris's body, laid out in its cardboard box in the bereavement room, a carpeted square of chairs, flowers, a lace tablecloth and a cross one of Chris's friends later hastily removed from the wall so as not to offend our collective atheism, wailed, "Baby, what have you done to yourself?" Then I fell upon him, his battered-with-death face, his stone hands. Uncomprehending. In grief, most absurdly and violently at the beginning, but capable of lingering on so much longer than I ever imagined following a loved one's death, one experiences a disjuncture.

The knowledge that this is a dead body, that this is the dead body of one's beloved, even the clear comprehension of how they died (a heart attack, a car accident) submerges itself beneath a childlike why, a voice that queries petulantly, anxiously or even in awe, "What has come to pass?" Writer Joan Didion calls this state a time of "magical thinking" in which one imagines that one's "thoughts or wishes had the power to reverse the narrative, change the outcome." In the weeks then months after Chris's death, I would come to experience the mind's capacity to torment, haunt and deceive me at a level I had never known before. But now I am still here, at the start of it all, staring down at him in what is not even a coffin as he is to be cremated. In fact, this is all they do here, at Simply Cremations, reduce loved bodies to ashes in their ovens, their cremulators.

Upon arrival at this squat building in one of Edmonton's many industrial districts, I am welcomed into a gaudy yet subdued office by a matronly young woman who smilingly presents me with forms and a Kleenex or two from one of the home's embossed metallic boxes. There are a ridiculous number of decisions to make. Choices that, however, keep my brain occupied, focused during this time of utter dispersal. Embalming or no? How many at the viewing? (A maximum of eight allowed if no embalming has taken place – by the orders of the Board of Health.) Do you want him dressed? (One hundred fifty dollars extra or they can leave him wrapped in his morgue sheet free of charge.) Is this a rush job? How many death certificates will you need? (The first four are included in the overall cost.) And then place a checkmark in this square, that one, the other one down there and again there, and how will you be paying? Your total today is $3,861.34. This total included the cheapest box, no embalming, two shellacked wooden urns, no other jewellery or commemorative plaques or wind chimes or sundials to contain the cremains in, that extra fee to dress him in camo pants and an Inhuman shirt, as well as to drape his silver grad chain around his solid neck. (No, I'm sorry, they inform me, but Doug the director will have to dress him. It's against the Health Board regulations for you to do so, the autopsy stitches are too wide, there could be leakage and so forth. We do hope you understand.) Oh, and several hundred dollars more for the rush job as we have to fly back to Vancouver the next day and thus he must be cremated tonight to give time, they tell us, for the ashes to cool prior to being bagged. I am to be denied many of what Arnold van Gennep refers to as "separation rituals," those that include "cleansing, anointing and purification," but at least I will be given time alone with him, and he will look, more or less, like himself, not clad in a sheet, not gussied up with blush, not hardened into a doll-corpse with embalming fluid. I am supposed to take solace in this.

Only two weeks ago, we spent our last night together in a motel room in Leduc. The Western Budget. The jacuzzi suite. Exhausted from lovemaking – truly it seemed that night we explored each other's flesh in every way we had ever longed for and were then spent, satisfied and yet wrung out, two lengths of material a giant hand had twisted with horrendous vigour, then dropped upon the sheets – we sat in bed quietly holding hands. Over the past few years, we had spoken little of his addiction. When I grew anxious, he would reassure me, "That won't happen again, baby. I nearly lost everything. I've learned my lesson! And besides, I didn't do it long enough to get really addicted. Don't worry, love." Following this recent bout with crack, however, these illusions, though sadly not the last of them, were gone. We spoke freely of his habit, watched documentaries, read books on addiction. He told me he had never forgotten the dealer's number, that he had seen a woman whose fingers had been cut off for drug debts, that he had smoked up to seventeen rocks in one thirty-hour period and had felt his heart race so insanely fast he was sure it was going to explode. "If I do it again, baby, I'll die, I know it," he said with great passion as we lay together that night, after eating Chinese food, watching the Al Pacino movie *Scent of a Woman*, which we had picked up earlier at Value Village, along with the final puzzle he would almost piece together before his death and those onyx pledge rings that we now wore on our fingers, provisional bands for eternal pledges. We had vowed to be there for each other, through everything, no more drugs for him, no further affairs for me, all honesty, all fidelity. (Frighteningly, a psychic I saw several months after he'd died, told me, "You gave him permission to do crack again with this pledge. Instead of making him prove himself over time, with few signs of his recovery, you essentially convinced his subconscious that anything he did from now on would be fine, because he had secured your love, which was, as you know, the most important thing in the world to him." So my commitment to him caused his death? How could I win in this case?)

When he said that, about dying the next time, I flung my head upon his smooth, bony chest, rested my ear against the *thum, thum, thum* and cried out, "Oh, your poor, poor heart! Your poor heart! Don't ever do that to it again, promise me." "I won't, sweetheart. I know now," he had replied, laying his hand upon my head, sliding it down the length of my hair, hair he loved to brush straight, exclaiming, "Pretty!" over its sleekness. Then he curled up with me, head beneath my chin, coiled his long limbs around mine and laughed, "We fit like Lego pieces!" Even after I saw him dead in his box at Simply Cremations, I believed him. I thought he had died of a heart attack, yes, but not one caused by any recently ingested drugs. Instead, I imagined it was due to a cumulative reaction, an unknown weakness in the organ, an unforeseen clot. It wasn't until I had recharged his cell phone and discovered that the last call he made was to Chainsaw, a dealer, not until after his truck was searched by my brother and crack found, that I knew he had fallen again and fallen finally, as he said he would.

A Complicated Death

When I first saw Chris's dead body, I was relieved, at least, that he hadn't died in a terrible car accident or been stabbed, shot or otherwise visually mutilated. His injuries were internal, hidden; his body and face hadn't been overtly harmed, and so I could see him again as he was, even though, by the fourth day, his skin was starting to bear decay's discolourations. Also, I tried to console myself that he hadn't been a wholly "innocent victim," but had been in some way complicit in his own end. Not in a consciously volitional manner, which even suicide isn't, but as a side effect of using crack. He wasn't killed by a stranger, at least, I thought at the beginning, or by his own driven hand, but by this third, intermediary condition; he acted in a way the rational brain knows is harmful and thus, as the puritanical voice at the back of the mind droned, "suffered the consequences." Even at the time of his death, after all we'd endured, I still didn't understand how, as Gabor Maté describes in his powerful book, *In the Realm of Hungry Ghosts*, drug addiction damages the decision-making processes in the brain, that the mind of someone drawn to such intense addictions has already been ruptured by early forms of abuse or a disruption in "emotional nurturance." I still thought he'd had a choice and could not comprehend why he had chosen as he did, given that his voice had been "happy" earlier that day – he had told me how much he missed me and we had spoken of the dreams we were starting, once again, to have.

When I tell people that Chris died at twenty-nine of a heart attack, the response is initially one of shock, then sympathy. "How could that happen?" people sigh. "So young!" And sometimes a jag of fear crosses their faces at the likelihood of such a death in their futures, at the inevitability of losing those they love, too. However, if I add, "He had become addicted to crack. Crack caused his heart attack and his death," then sympathy shifts, identification loosens. People suddenly feel this death won't happen to them, that they are different, that he was to blame, almost; that he deserved such an end after all the debts he'd created, the multiple stresses he had induced. Good riddance to what was merely another drain on the system, they may think. Even my own mother said to me, "His death was merciful because, well you know it was unlikely he would ever have gotten clean, and so he would have continued to cause himself, and others, pain. He would have destroyed you!" I know this is mostly true. And that it was said out of love. That, even with many bouts of rehab, the percentage of those who permanently stop using crack is frighteningly low. I also know that crack users, their personalities abducted by the drug, will lie, steal and commit other crimes to obtain their high. That watching a crack user eradicate him- or herself and those who remain faithful to them is one of the darkest visions ever created by humanity. And yet. I just wanted him back as he was. Before he became so depressed in my absence (and by numerous other shadowy factors that preceded and surmounted us) that he made that momentary move toward crack. A choice? An initial choice, at any rate, that is rapidly subsumed beneath a chemical compulsion, so that one becomes a machine of self-erasure, cloaked in a rabid hunger for elusive and illusionary pleasure.

The last words he said to me were "I love you, baby. I've never felt closer to you. I'll talk to you tomorrow. When you wake up, wake me up, too." And then he called his dealer. In the seemingly vast chasm between these two acts lives the addict. Their brains bear only minimal resemblances to ours at this point, we others who are still addicted, of course, but to lesser and more legal drugs like shopping or coffee or sex. We all crave acts that kick up our dopamine levels multiple times a day. Yet crack users do not have the rest of the day; their days, and their nights, are consumed by this relentless quest for another hit. All else that exists is eventually as nothing.

And yet I'm beginning to think that the grieving mind is possibly not that different from the drug-addicted mind. Didion herself comments on "the power of grief to derange the brain."

Grief has certainly ruptured my sense of place. When I'm in Edmonton now, I can never relax, anxious that I will run into someone from the past and will be unsettled anew. And grief does not end. Surging up, subsiding, rising in nearly fresh forms of suffering, sudden attacks, then hushing for a time, distancing, grief lives outside of any resolvable trajectories, easy resolutions. Grief intones that truth of non-return over and over again, arriving, as Didion describes, in "waves, paroxysms, sudden apprehensions . . . vortexes"; in what Roland Barthes defines as mourning's "discontinuous character." Yes, a year since Chris's death, I at least know this now: The stages of grieving are not five or seven or ten simple boxes of emotion, moving always toward acceptance, a letting go. No, there is nothing so defined about grief; it is its own organic force and it will hurl you into the well of yourself an endless number of times, hopefully with greater gentleness as the years pass. That is all you can ask for, really.

I have left Edmonton again, but the land where I became a widow remains, its magpie-flatness, cold-stunned earth, the tiniest of wildflowers waiting, how long they wait, to pierce through the grasses once more.

WORKS CITED

Barthes, Roland. *A Mourner's Diary*. New York: Hill & Wang, 2009.

Didion, Joan. *The Year of Magical Thinking*. New York: Alfred A. Knopf, 2005.

Maté, Gabor. *In the Realm of Hungry Ghosts: Close Encounters with Addiction*. Toronto: Vintage, 2009.

Oates, Joyce Carol. *A Widow's Story: A Memoir*. New York: HarperCollins, 2011.

Van Gennep, Arnold. *The Rites of Passage*. Moscow: University of Idaho, 1909.

FIVE:
FOREIGN REALMS

LIFE

Jane Eaton Hamilton

Just after she turned thirty-seven, at dinner, my mother said, "I have a gun. I'll keep it in my underwear drawer. If I get to forty, I mean it, I want you kids to get your hands on it and kill me."

"We're not going to kill you," said my big brother.

"I'm not kidding. I'm not turning forty! If I'm not dead –" She made a gun out of her fingers and pointed at her temple. "Kaboom!"

"Yeah, yeah," said my brother. And then, after a pause, "Can't you just do it yourself?"

I thought about that. My mother's intent. My mother's ability. She'd never followed through on her suicidal ideation, so we would actually have to kill her.

But it wouldn't be my brother who had to kill her. It would be me. It was always me. I was the one who got up to call the doctor when she brandished a butcher knife to off herself. If she made it to forty, she would toss her gun into my shaking hands, and if it hadn't already gone off, she'd stand there saying, *Shoot me, Janie, shoot me. Shoot me now. I said, do it. Do it. Do it.* And then I'd do it.

This is about grief.

One Easter when we were young, we woke to Easter baskets next to our beds, chocolate bunnies in a cellophane mess of pink nests, but also, when we crept to the hallway, a string and empty baskets. The three of us in our flannel jammies followed that web of string-ery wherever it took us, picking up Easter eggs at every directional change, down into the basement, into the living room, back to the root cellar, into the attic, into our parents' bedroom, into the kitchen, out the door to the porch, down along the path to the barn. We were too young to read; when we grew older, she changed our hunts from string to riddles, a tradition I carried down to my own kids.

This is about grief. About how a mother can show love rather than speak love.

Once at Hallowe'en, when my brother was twelve, she threw him a party. All afternoon she prepared spaghetti and grapes, carried them in bowls to her bedroom. She nailed sheets along the stairs at banister height so to get to the bathroom, you had to crawl rather than walk. She turned out all the lights, put on spooky music, guided the boys who arrived through the tunnel until a greeter, Scott's friend Mike, led them to the bowls – the spaghetti was now veins, the grapes were eyeballs, pretzels were rat tails and a sponge was a brain.

She was so creative, my mother, so that one of the locations of my grief is her hands. But here is another:

When my parents separated, my mother left my brother and sister in Canada with Dad and moved me down to the Bahamas, where for the first time I fell in love with the world, spilling myself carelessly into the ocean, coming up sputtering, riding rattletrap bikes barefoot to my one-room schoolhouse, taking lessons on warmed rocks in the sunshine while newborn yellow chicks peeped past. I had a friend, too: Margo. I spent every night sleeping over at her house, her mother taking me in when my own mother wanted to be with her lover.

For decades after leaving the Caribbean, I had nightmares where I couldn't get back, where I was exiled to Canada, to snow and cold. Swamps stood in my way; men aimed machine guns at me; snapping animals tried to eat me.

All I ever wanted was to get back home. Why couldn't I go back? My friends were there, Margo and a boy named Luther.

This is about locations of grief.

After her breakup, my mother spiralled. She'd always been hooked on Mother's Little Helpers, but now she doctor-hopped, getting the same prescriptions from multiple physicians.

My mother would arrange her daily pills in a circle. I never counted them, but perhaps in those bad, too-stoned years spanning my adolescence, there were forty to fifty, a thick circle twelve to fifteen inches wide. Uppers and downers and in-betweeners. She'd swallow them in handfuls with water. She was so stoned she slumped into her upholstered chair and let her cigarettes burn to the filter without remembering to take a puff. I pulled cigarette after burned-down cigarette from between her chapped lips, tossed them into ashtrays before the grey snakes slithered into her lap. Time after time her chair smouldered and I'd find her slumped over smoke. Its stuffing kept bursting into flame. It was pockmarked with the wet black gullies. She put us all at risk.

This is about locations of grief.

When I reached adulthood, my mother moved to the US to care for her father, and after his death, stayed illegally and refused to cross back into Canada. I was able to fly south only twice, where I was flabbergasted to witness her, tender and engaged with my children, instead of stoned and incapable.

Even after Mom signed up for amnesty, she never came north.

My mother had actively fought racism when we were children; it was one of the things I most admired about her. But in Florida, all the nits of her dormant white racism hatched at the same time, and she became an infestation of right-wing hatred. I would try, in phone call after phone call, to reach her, to slash through her -isms, and even though I dreaded her launching into stories, lethal as knives, about women or Haitian refugees or gay people, letting her impugn me/us, when I finally, softly, said, horrified, "Mom, that's racist," she would refuse to take my call again for months.

I could have my mother if I showed myself to be racist, but if I continued to fight racism, I couldn't have my mother.

My sister in Florida was no better. When she married, Sally invited me and the kids to her wedding, but not my butch partner. I was non-binary. Sally wanted me to "stand with her," but warned that I would have to shave, legs and armpits, wear a dress and, she said, "Behave. Anyone seeking to ruin my special day will be frowned upon." By what, I wanted to cry out, seducing a bridesmaid? By telling the truth of who I was?

This is about locations of grief.

Ontario. The Bahamas. Florida, where I spent much time. I had almost seen the Apollo 11 launch in 1969 at Cape Canaveral, but the car had broken down partway there. I'd driven the strip in Miami. I'd glided over manatees. I'd swum with dolphins. I'd thrown fish into the mouths of pelicans.

I was delighted in 2003 when, at seventy-two, her long-ago demand to kill her no doubt forgotten on her side, my mother got her own computer and Internet so that I'd be able to email her without others looking over her shoulder. But it was just then, putting up a shelf before our first communiqué, that she fell. My siblings didn't see fit to tell me, or tell me, either, about her hospitalization for knee surgery. The first thing I heard was that she'd died, likely from poor anticoagulation and a blood clot.

The shock of the sudden death. The inglorious slap of reality across the face. The realization of finality.

But Mom's death or funeral are not what I want to talk about, though Mom's ashes, as they silted through the ocean over a coral reef in the sunshine off Key Largo, caught the light like jewels.

*

When I returned to Vancouver from her funeral, my grief was furious, unhinged. Did it help me to know my suffering was as common as all grief, that its very certainty made it banal? No. My experience of it was profound, even if, intellectually, I could examine it under a magnifier and pronounce it lucky that my mother had gone quickly without suffering or, on our purely selfish side, medical bills. I wondered, after two parents instantly dead (my father of suicide when I was a teen), what it would have been like to care for an elderly, ill parent, with a chance to adapt to what was coming, an opportunity to say the things that needed to be said? Yet the important part, the wound, was that she was gone, and all the tendrils that snaked from it – the trouble of her possessions, of splitting her minor assets, of fairness, the altering of family dynamics, the regrets – were all that was left.

I'd been in the middle of getting my certification as a Master Gardener when she died, and I finished but my MG certification sagged into uselessness. I'm an atheist, but for a solid year, only in my house, I walked into patches of adult-sized smoke I couldn't see but could smell. I was a down-trodden cliché, slumping though my days, admonishing myself for not trying harder with Mom. (I'd been arranging a trip with my girls for June, but she died in February. I was actually contemplating going to see her a few weeks before she died, when some money came in, but I would have had to go alone, and I was nervous of driving because of a rash of Florida violence perpetrated on those who rented cars.) My guilt swamped me.

*

I became that person who would have – yes, seriously, like everyone else, as common as coffee – traded everything for even five more telephone minutes, recriminations and all. I hadn't made her feel welcomed in my life, or loved.

I had long been a litigant in Canada's same-sex marriage case; unexpectedly, just following Mom's demise, the prohibition against queers marrying fell and my intended and I were able to wed after five years engaged, an exultation. We had both lost our mothers during our extended court case, something that wouldn't have happened to heterosexuals able to marry when they wanted. My mother, a nurse, sewer and baker whose homophobia had been wavering, might have agreed to make our cake. My wife's mother, also a homophobe, would certainly have been at our side regardless.

Isn't this how it goes, in particularly intense years? A windfall like the changed constitution, the rug pulled out simultaneously with a parent's death?

Utterly unexpected: after my mother died, and I didn't have to deal with her reality, I fell in love with her. I didn't merely discover I'd loved her – had I? Lifelong, I'd had no recall of it – but I fell in love with her with the same intensity I'd fallen for romantic partners (minus, of course, the sexual aspects).

Had she ever loved me? As a newborn, I'd had pyloric stenosis; whenever she fed me, I projectile vomited. I doubt she ever bonded with a screaming, famished infant. When I was a toddler, I liked to pour a mess of sand in my hair any chance I got for the pleasure of scratching it out. Once, I wandered away from the sandbox, and after being unable to find me for a day, firemen and police announced I'd likely drowned in our pond, though I was actually safe, just not found. For years afterward, when I went outside, she often hollered, "Don't drown again!" I had alopecia totalis at six, an embarrassment (Mom never stopped goading me about being ugly, she was so embarrassed). My brother was her boy. My sister was her golden child. I was just a . . . tomboy with scruffy, cropped hair.

Her mental health continued its steady decline. Stoned, she still had her rare charming moments; I lived for them, nourished myself from them, but they did not elicit my love.

To fall in love with Mom when I no longer had to protect myself from her cruelties was revelatory. It was the core of the love I had loved when developing in her womb, or as a newborn, before we'd been separated by my incubator, before my love gathered its significant or petty conditions and limitations.

The year after Mom's death, I flew my family to Andros Island in the Bahamas where I had lived with my mother in 1963. I had not been back in decades. The place we'd lived in still existed, and the one-room schoolhouse where I was educated remained, converted to a church. I still loved Andros. We picked our way across rocks and let the hot wind batter us to scatter more of Mom's ashes; this time, in the actual spots she had walked and loved. Everything here was the same as it had been for that time when I had my mother all to myself – no sister, no brother vying for her attention, when she had been happy; that day, I bought a sterling ring with a shell design that I still wear to link me back to her, and to Andros, and to love.

Back in Vancouver, I learned to love her through roses and lilacs, her flowers. A horticultural friend cultured a rose he named after her: Wacky Sheila. I planted it, and as it grew, I thought of her; as I cut her flowers for vases, she bloomed anew in my heart, the young, happy woman of Andros.

But I also thought of the long-ago promise she'd extracted from me and my siblings to kill her at forty. By the time forty had come, I'd forgotten the promise. Instead, right then, I was pregnant and horrified by the restrictive abortion laws in Canada. I needed my mother like I'd never needed her before. I remember her fortieth birthday sliding by virtually unremarked.

But that's another story, isn't it? Being pregnant and sorry at seventeen, having a mother who did or didn't agree to help? Another location of grief?

MY SISTER IN NEW YORK CITY

James Picard

Everything, and I do mean everything, is subject to impermanence. There are no certainties. Everything that comes together will eventually fall apart, everything that goes up will come down and life always ends in death. No exceptions. We all hope for a long and healthy time on the planet, though there is no guarantee. We are told throughout life to plan for our future, as if it is certain that we all will live to a ripe old age somewhere in our seventies, eighties or even nineties. But, as I've come to realize, this is a fallacy like so many others that we have been taught. I came to the realization of life's impermanence when I was nineteen years old. That is the gift that my sister, Catherine, gave to me when she died at twenty-one. When someone dies young it helps to teach this lesson; the trick is to keep it in the forefront of your mind . . . constantly, so that it takes hold and you truly learn from it. My sister was not ill or suicidal. She was not in an accident and her death, unfortunately, was not instantaneous. She was murdered, her youthful and vibrant life taken from her in a random act of violence.

I am an artist by vocation, and creating my art has always been a struggle. I had little support for my talents, except from my sister. Her encouragement kept me going, even after my works were burned in our fireplace at the hands of our father, and my high school art teachers failed me as I never did exactly as I was told. I knew I had something that no one could extinguish, and most of all I had someone who believed in me. That all changed, however, when the police showed up at my door in early November of 1983. I was notified that my sister had been discovered deceased in New York City two months into my first year at art college. The two officers, holding their hats by their side, both said they were sorry for my loss and handed me a card with phone numbers to call on it.

I was my sister's next of kin – we both left home as young teenagers to escape my father's violence. We were like two war veterans who'd survived together, bonded by the experience of trauma. We even attempted to stop the violence as young children by slitting my father's throat while he slept. Unfortunately, he woke up just as the knife held in both our hands started to puncture his skin. We ran for our lives and lived to share that story and many others as we got older. We became inseparable as young adults. But that closeness came to an abrupt end on November 3, 1983. I had to come to terms with the fact that my best friend, sibling and fellow childhood trauma survivor was no longer with me on the planet.

New York City was the art capital of the world after the end of World War II. It was the place to go if you were an artist. It contained the best galleries, the best art collections, the best art schools and the best art exhibitions in the world.

It was always a place I saw myself in, wandering the streets, visiting museums and being inspired. I had been there only once before, when I was nearly eighteen, and I absolutely fell in love with the city that never sleeps. I was heading there now for the second time, but circumstances were much different. I was there to identify my sister's body in the morgue and to make arrangements for her body and belongings to be returned to Canada. The city, this time, seemed different . . . colder, greyer and much less friendly. It had lost its "shine" for me, like everything else in the world. I realized then that things would never be the same. I knew now that my art was the only thing I could count on, and decided then and there to embrace it with every ounce of energy I had in me for however long I had left on this planet.

I stepped out of the cab and took a deep breath, climbed the stairs and opened the door at the top that would lead me to be reunited with my sister.

The people inside seemed genuine and caring, and offered me a coffee, which I could not drink due to the nausea I had felt since arriving. I waited on a chair in the waiting room to be escorted to the morgue. I don't recall how I got from the waiting area to a room with a window; I felt numb, both physically and mentally, and everything seemed surreally quiet. On the other side of the glass was a gurney with a sheet pulled over something that resembled a human body. I approached the window, and the officer who stood by my side nodded to the man in the lab coat who was standing by my sister's covered corpse. He very slowly and gently pulled back the sheet and I heard a voice, which seemed so very distant, ask me if the body was that of my sister. I did not reply and was asked again in a much softer tone. I remember a hand on my shoulder, but still I could not get the words to come out. I knew it was her, but her face was badly bruised and I wanted to make sure by looking a little longer. I also didn't want to say the word "yes" as it would then allow reality to hit me like a sledgehammer and snap me out of this surreal fog I had been in for three days and counting. Eventually, I succumbed to the fact that, yes that indeed was her, and I managed to nod my head and give a muffled yes. The sheet was pulled over her once again and I was escorted back upstairs where I was given a small envelope that contained a pair of red teardrop earrings. Most of her belongings had been stolen and what was left was being held as evidence. I hung onto those earrings as if my life depended on it. It was all I had now . . . well, that and my art . . . and my memories.

I woke up the next day in my hotel room. I had barely slept but remember looking out the window and seeing the sun. I was alive. I took a deep breath: yes, I was breathing and had the entire day ahead of me to breathe. I also had something that those who were recently deceased did not have: I had opportunity. The opportunity to live my life fully and completely. It is something that you can miss out on because we, as a society, have built life around the illusion of living forever. We think we have all the time in the world, but actually, in fact, we don't. We have just as much life as is given to us before we all die.

From that day forward, I vowed to remember and honour the life that I have been given. I decided to never forget that breath I took in the hotel room after visiting my sister in the morgue and I never did. If I go to sleep, I wake up with that exact same feeling I had on that chilly but sunny early November morning in New York City. I said "if I go to sleep" because there are days and nights that I fill so fully and completely with my existence that I do not sleep, and as I promised myself, that if it was indeed my last day on earth, I can truly say I got the very utmost out of that twenty-four-hour day . . . a full twenty-four hours. I have lived the past thirty-six-and-a-half years of my life since then the way I've wished to live. I have painted and drawn continuously throughout that time; I have travelled and spent a large majority of my life helping others by being a kind, caring and compassionate human who follows his truth always. I feel I owe that to my sister, Catherine, but also to all those wonderful human beings who have left the planet too soon and never got to achieve their full potential. Isn't that what life is all about? I live my life as one who has survived, and in surviving I can keep alive the hopes and dreams of the many who are not here.

Because everything is subject to impermanence and there are no certainties. The realization of life's impermanence . . . it truly is a gift. Life imparts lessons to us continually and one of the greatest of all, I feel, is death.

FOR YOUR READING AND COLLECTING PLEASURE

Lisa Richter

Cuba, 2004. My then boyfriend and I save up our dollars, pack our bags and, despite an almost comical series of setbacks, including a crippling bout of laryngitis (on my part) and a misplaced passport (on his), make it to Varadero. I stroll the grounds of our resort in a state of disbelief. Leafy-green light, white sand beaches, the bath-warm sea's myriad shades of blue. Unlimited mojitos at makeshift beach bars with thatched roofs. On the hotel room bed, crisp white towels sculpted into the shape of two swans with entwined necks, embracing. Flashy, yet admittedly fun nighttime entertainment. A life-size chess game we play at night. The decadence of the all-inclusive, everything smooth on the surface, a manufactured paradise.

And so it goes, our relaxing, beach-lounging, indulging in the mildly tedious yet requisite trappings, a mid-twenties couple on vacation. Most of the other couples at the resort are Canadian. A few Europeans. One of the women I speak to, with long pink fingernails and straightened ash-blonde hair, speaks of getting "pre-tanned."

A few days into our trip, my mother calls our hotel room phone and tells me my grandfather is dying.

In his poem "Beyond Beginnings," after the loss of his wife, Michiko, the poet Jack Gilbert writes:

The Aegean
was blue just then at the end of the valley,
and is blue now differently.

The Caribbean Sea is my Aegean. The lushness of the landscape, the cobbled-together vintage cars, the musicality of Spanish in the nearby village we visit on a rented scooter: all of it shrouded in a daze of anticipatory grief.

I travel to Montreal by train with my mother to bury my grandfather a few weeks later. My grandmother doesn't wear black to the funeral. She sits in silence during the memorial service at Paperman & Sons, her hands folded in her lap in front of her. Even at the burial site, as members of the immediate family take turns shovelling dirt onto the casket, customary at Jewish funerals, Grandma stands back, her face blank, unreadable, her round blue eyes blurred behind the thick lenses of her glasses. My mother clutches my arm, weeping softly.

"Well, it's over now," says my grandmother. No one asks what, exactly, is over: the funeral itself, my grandfather's life, their six decades together or the especially difficult last few years of it, in which she cared for a husband as he recovered from a severe stroke. I wonder if a small part of her is not relieved that he's gone. Her voice has a flatness to it, a blunt edge, like a rock beaten by wave after wave until it fades and softens, unable to inflict injury or pain.

*

In my last memory of my grandfather, less than six months before his death, he is eating chicken soup, listening to Shostakovich on the radio in the kitchen of my grandparents' three-bedroom condominium in Côte-Saint-Luc. Tears sluice down his cheeks as he struggles to sing the melody and conduct, his gnarled, liverspotted hands trembling as they hover and dip in the air. My grandmother smiles and laughs, almost nervously. "He cries a lot now," she explains to me.

Granddad's stroke has changed him. The man who used to grin and call my sister and me "lady" when we were little. Who, with a fine fountain pen, in beautiful cursive script, would inscribe the hardcover editions of classics from his own library that he gave us as presents: "For your reading and collecting pleasure." Walt Whitman's *Leaves of Grass*. *Sister Carrie*. *Great Expectations*. *The Collected Works of Thomas Paine*. Books that stood in gold-edged refinement, in stark contrast to the yellow-paged, dog-eared paperbacks that crammed our shelves, my father's old spy novels and historical fiction, my mother's collections of short stories, poetry and drama. Henry Miller. James Joyce. Philip Roth. An adult novel of Judy Blume's that I snuck away into my bedroom in grade six.

My mother has a framed black-and-white photograph of my grandparents as a young married couple, taken somewhere in Europe, in front of a nameless cathedral. My grandfather is not conventionally handsome, but so striking with his strong features, slicked back dark hair and distinctive cleft chin, which I have inherited. In the photograph, he is, as always, impeccably dressed. His heavy, black-framed glasses add weight and seriousness to his youthful face. He holds his wife by the elbow, a light but firm grip: ushering, escorting. My grandmother is lovely in a sleeveless floral dress, most likely made by the seamstress who made all her dresses, Mrs. Rozanov. She peers at the camera with a smile that suggests mild embarrassment. Awkwardness in front of cameras runs in my family.

In other photos I remember from my grandparents' condominium, my grandfather stands in a Montreal office or boardroom. There are framed newspaper clippings from the opening of Montreal's Place Bonaventure, interviews from the *Montreal Gazette*. He was known to be ruthless in business, a fierce debater, an erudite patron of the arts, a self-styled intellectual. A member of the Communist Party of Canada (allegedly blacklisted in the States during the McCarthy era), early NDP supporter, civil rights advocate and staunch atheist, having renounced the Orthodox Judaism of his childhood. My mother, an artist and writer herself, recalls political meetings in her childhood home, folk music hootenannies and coffee houses, protest songs, anti-nuke rallies: the stuff leftist legends are made of.

After I moved to Montreal for university in the mid-'90s, I spent more time with my grandparents and made a point of getting to know them better. With each visit, we grew closer, chipping away at the estrangement and detachment that I had absorbed from my father, who'd had a strained, complicated relationship with his in-laws from the start. Eager to please my father as a child, I sided with him when he expressed his unmasked contempt. Ironically, what my father despised most in his father-in-law were the qualities they both shared:

unspeakably strong convictions, outspokenness and near-unbreakable stubbornness.

After my grandfather's death in 2004, my grandmother continues to live alone in their condominium. She calls me to tell me about an arts programs on Bravo she thinks I'd like, sends me articles clipped from newspapers on everything from the anti-aging properties of green tea to groan-worthy Yiddish jokes. Some months later, with worsening health, she moves into a nursing home. I take the bus back to Montreal to see her. She introduces me proudly to her fellow residents, compliments me on my clothes, my dark blue nail polish. A few weeks go by before my grandmother falls and a breaks a hip, dying a few days later.

I return to Montreal once or twice a year now, mostly to visit friends. Most trips find me wandering the same streets I wandered while living there as a student in the '90s, in neighbourhoods steeped in personal and familial history. I walk past the new vape stores, cafés and clothing boutiques on St-Laurent where my paternal grandfather's butcher shop opened six decades ago. I walk by the triplex on St-Denis, south of Mont-Royal, where my granddad was born and raised. A plain bedsheet hangs across the front window. I walk up through Mile End, where Hasidic Jews and their sprawling families speaking Yiddish rekindle the days of my grandparents' childhood, the Eastern European shtetl, a thriving culture destroyed by the Holocaust.

Grief is known for having its own whims and desires, prone to coming and going at odd hours, leading in unknown directions, ending in dark, secluded groves, tree trunks rough and bare where sunlight fails to reach. It reaches me when I least expect it, as I stop in and out of thrift and used bookstores on my way up to visit my friend Kelly, north of Bernard, east of Parc. Though over the last twenty-plus years I have made Montreal my own, it remains a city of ghosts. Both sets of grandparents are now gone. I think of my parents in their youth, of my father growing up in what he described as the "working-class neighbourhood" of Snowdon, and eventually the leafy suburb of Côte-Saint-Luc. I picture my newlywed parents, only twenty years old when they married in 1968, walking hand in hand along these streets. In Montreal, I am blindsided by nostalgia for my own childhood memories, too: our almost-yearly trips to visit relatives over Passover; the warm bagels we bought fresh out of the oven at Fairmount or St-Viateur, and of course, my father's near-carnal love of Schwartz's smoked meat.

Absence has a palpable weight. I feel my grandparents' absence bearing down on my chest, accompanied by another sensation: the unmistakable pangs of guilt and regret, for once allowing my father's perception of my grandparents to become my own. I pause and breathe until the guilt passes, considering how relationships with grandparents are so often less complicated than those with parents, especially if, as in my case, they lived hundreds of kilometres away. How so often we love people with a dumb, senseless intensity, even if, or perhaps because, we barely know them.

Toronto, February 2018. I am living with my fiancé Stéphane (several relationships after my Cuba companion) in the Christie Pits neighbourhood. We have been engaged over a year; our wedding is only four months away. My father emails me from Hamburg, where he's been staying with friends for the past few months, to tell me he's coming home for a visit and to renew his Russian visa: for years, he's been living in Moscow with his second wife. He tells me he will be arriving in Toronto on February 14. It's been almost a year since the last time I've seen him, though it was only supposed to be a month. After many years of broken promises, it is hard to take his word at face value, yet I do and start to make plans to have him stay with us on our couch. And though Stéphane and I have never been the kind of couple to make much of a fuss out of Valentine's Day, for some reason, this year it seems important to me, as if my father's impending arrival were deliberately planned to cramp our style. We go out for dinner and celebrate Valentine's Day on the thirteenth instead.

February 14 is a surprisingly mild, sunny day. I try on wedding dresses in a Kensington Market vintage store after work, thinking of what I'll make for my father to eat when he arrives from the airport. Later that night, we pass the time watching *Star Trek: Deep Space Nine* on Netflix, waiting for my father. We wait and wait. We make up the couch with sheets and blankets. I try calling and emailing: *Dad, where are you? I'm getting worried.* No response. We run through logical explanations: He missed his connecting flight. He got lost. His phone is dead. He took a taxi to a hotel instead *(why? and how could he afford it?)* and will call us in the morning. We finally go to bed, barely sleeping, listening for the buzzer downstairs. As I fall asleep, I think of calling hospitals in the morning *(or the police?)*. I tell myself I'm overreacting. Everything will be fine.

At six in the morning, the phone rings.

It is Roland, my father's friend and host in Hamburg, Germany.

In his polite, clipped English, he says, "I am very sorry to tell you that the reason your father did not arrive last night. He had an aneurysm on the train on the way to the airport in Frankfurt, and he died in the hospital a few hours later."

Toronto, August 2019. For a long time, I did not want to release this memoir about my grandparents. How could I publish a piece about grief and loss, I asked myself, coming from such a place of naïveté? Only three months after I finished it, I lost my father. How could I write about my grandparents' deaths, however sad and difficult and painful, no matter how much I loved them and missed them, after the most devastating loss of my life? The tragedy of my father's death: alone, in a foreign country, on his way home to see his family, at the age of sixty-nine, was too impossibly hard to write an essay about. I had no insights, no wisdom, no way to make narrative sense of it all. All I wanted to say: *Dad, fuck you for dying. Dad, I miss you. Dad, I'm sorry.*

A year and a half later, when I tell people my story, I can keep my voice calm and even, though I inevitably reach a point in the story when I feel my throat growing raspy and closing, and feel a cry welling up in my chest. I hold it in, hold it down and keep telling. I tell anyone who will listen. My therapist speaks to me about complicated bereavement, how hard it is when loss is sudden and unexpected, when we are unable to say goodbye. I cry sometimes when I hear the Beatles songs my father loved, or songs from the opera *Carmen* that

I grew up listening to. He loved so much wonderful music. My father appears in my dreams and my poems, ever the self-inviting guest. I am now married to a man I love with my whole heart. He remembers my father well. We talk about him often, about his many confounding and maddening contradictions, his eccentricities, his outrageous "dad jokes" and, despite everything, his absolute love and dedication.

More than any geographical site, I have heard that grief is located in the body. How does one excise grief, separate oneself from what is so deeply embedded? Does grief cannibalize the self, subsume it completely, or does the self continue to exist as an autonomous entity, irrevocably altered by it? For a long time, I wanted no part of the healing advocated by the mainstream self-help literature. A year and a half after my father's death, I am not, nor do I aspire to be "over it." There's a strange, unexpected comfort in the knife-edge of despair, the feeling of its ice-cold blade against my cheek, my new familiar. And yet, with time, the pain ebbs more forgivingly. It can return in an instant, yet those instants are further and further apart.

I think back to Tess Gallagher's lines in her poem "Now That I Am Never Alone" in her gorgeous collection *Moon Crossing Bridge,* written after losing her husband, the writer Raymond Carver: "But I remember solitude – no other / presence and each thing what it was." One morning, about a month after my father's death, I stepped outside. It was a piercingly bright, early spring day. There was still snow on the ground. I breathed in the cold, fresh air. The feeling was euphoric. I had not expected this. That amidst the unbearable suffering, or perhaps in counterpoint to it, I could experience intense, radiant bursts of joy. I was alive! The sky was blue! The purity of that single moment, unadulterated, was stop-in-your-tracks-and-gasp beautiful. *Each thing was what it was.*

I am not one to speak of silver linings, nor one to suggest that everything has a reason. And yet, for better or worse, I cannot compare the person I am today with the person I was then, before my father died. I do not necessarily like her better, only recognize that she has acquired a certain perspective that has rendered her more attuned, perhaps, and certainly more appreciative of all sorts of pleasures. The pleasure of reading and collecting books, and sharing them with others. The pleasure of sobbing: the horrific pain's dramatic purging. The understanding that nothing is the same, nor can I expect it to be. Not a consolation or comfort but a continuation, a consistency. A continuum.

WE ARE STILL HERE: J.S. BACH'S VIOLIN PARTITA NO. 2 IN D MINOR, BWV 1004

Theresa Kishkan

The leading British conductor and Bach scholar Christopher Hogwood, who in 1973 founded the Academy of Ancient Music with its mission to play Baroque music on period instruments, tells me that he's puzzled by students coming his way who, for instance, play minuets every day of their lives without knowing how to dance a minuet.
– Philip Clark, "Deconstructing the Genius of Bach," *Limelight Magazine*

1. *Allemanda,* in Toulouse, on Mount Tolmie

The opening, grave and ominous.

My mother has been dead for seven years. I've been working on a book about family history – hers, in part, though mostly my father's mother's history in Horní Lomná, in what's now the Czech Republic. Most days I find myself thinking about the strange and wonderful cartography of motherhood, across seas and generations, the maps imaginary and remote. How *my* mother's mother was unknown to her

– my mum was given up at birth to a foster home and raised to think of herself as motherless – and how that first terrible loss shaped her, blank area on the map. She told a granddaughter once that she'd only ever wanted to be a mother, as though she needed to fill the emptiness of herself with that function, scribble her place in geography. When I was young, it never seemed enough to me. I wanted more of her, from her. But now I realize – too late – what she gave me and my brothers.

In Toulouse, last March, I dreamed of my mother. I'd been thinking a great deal about geographical loneliness. Not only for a place one has left, often forever (my grandmother never returned to Europe and, as far as I know, had only very sporadic contact with her family there), but also the loneliness we feel when we try to follow the traces our ancestors left across a landscape. A map, on paper or in memory; a field loved by a child for its birdsong; the scent of plum blossom after a long winter; a tree planted to celebrate a wedding, a birth, an occasion long forgotten. So, the dream of my mother surprised me. She was on a guided tour, just before heart surgery. I always wanted to travel to France, she said, her eyes glowing as she jostled and joked with her new friends, but no one would ever go with me. She had photographs – a long road pink with oleander leading down to the sea, a restaurant filled with sunlight, a plate of sausage. (As far as I know, she never used a camera.) I held her hand and thought, I have another chance. We went to the restroom together and she was running. Please, Mum, don't run, I pleaded with her only half in fun. Please. I don't want you to die on me!

(Walk three steps, then lift a foot. 2/4 time.)

Now I wish I'd offered to take her to France, though I wonder if she truly wanted to go or if the dream came from my own pleasure at the sight of umbrella pines, orange trees, the silvery leaves of olives. She confessed once, after my father died, that she'd always hoped to go to Greece. I looked at her with such surprise, I remember, because the trips she took were to Reno or Disneyland and, once, to Hawaii. Packaged tours, on buses or charter flights. Later she and my father travelled to places he'd been to in the Navy and insisted she'd love: Singapore, Hong Kong, Thailand. I don't think she did love those trips, but my father was persuasive.

I have a photo album sent to her after her foster sister died. Mostly it's a record of her foster sister's life, but there are a few early photographs of my mum, aged three, in a garden, or standing by some stairs. She is chubby and dark haired. So far away in time, in geography – she grew up in Halifax. But somehow curiously present, her clear eyes, her smile. ("Thou art thy mother's glass, and she in thee . . ." Her eyes, in mine. Her knees, with that migrating pain. At the end of her life, she could barely walk.)

Until her death, I don't believe I ever danced an allemanda. A linear movement in binary form. Walk three steps, then lift a foot. 2/4 time. Four couples, her children and their partners, promenading the length of her living room in an apartment on the slope of Mount Tolmie, entwining their arms as one lifts a box of her photographs (though no shots of France), another passes a load of her clothing (the cardigans, the polyester trousers, the tiny socks, a few threadbare nightdresses) and the remaining dancers keep their place in the movement. There is nothing French in the apartment, no music, but what I hear in my head as I step, as I sort, as I turn, turn, the old harmonies returning.

From Toulouse, lift, lift, make a place in your arms for a
mother who ran like a girl to rejoin her friends who waited
in France, who watched deer make their own graceful steps
below her window on Mount Tolmie, lace your arms with
hers, turn, turn, toward her, away. Careful with your knees as
you lift each foot, stand where she stood, 2/4 time, the years
passing before the window, like the deer.

**2. *Corrente*, BC Cancer Agency, 600 West 10th Avenue,
Vancouver, BC, with longing, with expectation**

Quick step through the generous doors, quick step to the
right where the sign points to Functional Imaging. Quick,
quick, while you can, while the notes are tied, delicate.

When I entered, there was silence. Four or five people
on chairs, one in a hospital smock, one man with an elegant
leather handbag holding his mother's hand. I was asked
to briefly sit and then was invited into a room where a
technologist injected me with radioactive sugar to act as a
tracer in my body. What music would you like? he asked as
he covered me with a warm flannel blanket and dimmed the
lights. And Bach was my request. Violin accompanied me for
sixty minutes as I closed my eyes and thought about my life,
the life I loved and that might be changing.

Having heard the *Quirks & Quarks* show on meditation,
I'm pretty sure I wasn't meditating. I thought of the Venus
of Laussel, a limestone bas-relief sculpture I saw a few years
ago in Bordeaux. She dates from 29,000–22,000 BCE and
has traces of red ochre on her breasts and abdomen. When
I saw her, I knew her. There's nothing fashionable about her
body. She's full and abundant. She's one of a group of female
figures from the paleolithic period, and although there's some

debate about what she's holding – a horn of plenty? a symbol of a woman's lunar cycles? (there are thirteen lines inscribed in the shape) – I think it's clear that she's a fertility symbol. A woman who has likely borne children and has known good meals, who has probably even provided them, from her own body and ingenuity.

She was a good companion for me during that part of the procedure. And when I had to lie on the narrow plank and enter the long cylinder for the scan itself – it took twenty minutes – I closed my eyes and thought of her again. It helped immensely to have her present. I brought to my mind's eye my husband and my children, their partners, my three grandchildren. Then I visualized each of my books, their thirteen titles in lines across my inner vision. My eyelids fluttered with effort and I almost cried. I was afraid if I opened my eyes, I would be nothing. I would be someone with radioactive glucose in her body and possibly something worse. But the goddess, her face absent of features but her body so complex and whole, stayed with me the whole time, her horn in her right hand. My hand flexed in time.

I was still inside the cylinder, still as a person sleeping, or dead. Eyes closed, mind filled with the beauty of my family, the binary forms I'd grown in my body – two sons, a daughter, each of them in turn born with undeveloped sperm or egg cells, contributions to the grandchildren who were oblivious to their grandmother still on a bench in the imaging scanner, their great-grandparents hovering, too. And theirs. Impossibly light but all-powerful, prehistoric limestone, feathery penniform to her right, her wide buttocks and hips flaring as mine flared under the blue cotton smock, my companion in the ceremonial cave where her horn was the thing that kept us steady together as we waited to learn if my cells were absorbing the glucose, if malignancies were hidden in my chest and torso.

The Venus gently pushed my foot to propel me back into the room, her hand surprisingly firm as it reached out of the stone, tapped her horn to my heels. There you are, go back! And when I came out of the cylinder, it was like being reborn. Sort of. I thought of John Berger's observations about the Chauvet Cave: "Step outside the cave and re-enter the wind-rush of time passing. Reassume names. Inside the cave, everything is present and nameless. Inside the cave, there is fear, but the fear is in perfect balance with a sense of protection."[1]

Time now to take off the blue smock, put on your day clothes, two steps and then a double (single/single/double) to the left, then repeating the same to the right (heel blessed by the goddess) with single or double straight steps, a little skip as you leave the suite of rooms where you have been wrapped in warm flannel, sent into the cave (single, single, though your loved ones hovered). In the waiting room and the hall at the cancer clinic, you see the dancers moving slowly on the polished linoleum, two steps, a careful double, repeat, repeat, their wheelchairs and walkers, their canes and the arms of those who help to support them, the final bars of the corrente slowed down, slowed for those waiting for procedures, for leaving the imaging rooms, the rooms where the chemicals are dripped into veins, the beauty of the dance, theirs for time suspended in the dust motes, "clearly music on which hopes are built,"[2] the bright lights overhead, the little groups huddled on benches, heads down in sorrow, hands clasped in fear.

3. *Sarabanda,* from the Beskydy Mountains to old age on a porch in Edmonton

Stately, sweetly slow, take me there, one step, the stressed second.

A choreography of distance, a small wooden house in a tiny village in the Beskydy Mountains holding the girlhood of my father's mother, spruce trees along the road in front and the slope of the mountains behind. Fruit trees in snow. The sound of church bells. Plum blossom following the deep snow, the return of sheep from sheds to the new grass. Stately slow, the ancient transhumance of sheep and their shepherds, a migration from one ridge of the Carpathians to the Beskydys, in snow, in sunlight. A poke in the ribs, slow, slow, the grazing, the arrivals in far pastures. As my grandmother walked, slow, with her children, one a baby wrapped in a shawl, in the snow on the road away from the village.

A slow triple, one step, a stressed second, age slowing the limbs in space, where is the foot, where is the knee that bent to potatoes, to the tiny chicks newly hatched, where the arm in relation to the body, muscles firmed by laundry, the garden, rolling out dough for noodles she sold at the door, now gone. Gone the door, the batten walls. Where is the photograph of Julia's funeral, chick grown to rooster, caught by the camera and children posed in the clothing they wore to Mass. Where is the husband, dead also. And an earlier daughter, buried in the cemetery above the town.

Dust in summer. Cold wind off the river in winter. No one wanted the work of potatoes, saving bags for dill seed, no one wanted to cut noodles by hand when the market sold them in cellophane bags. Step, step, slow as the melting of snow, the passing of time. In a chair on a porch, tap your feet to old melodies, someone tuning a fiddle in a warm room while the men drank slivovice and dreamed of making their fortunes in the New World. The Roma have come with their own strange instruments, battered drums, a horn of burnished apricot wood, their horses tied to the gate. The dancing that night was wild, every step returned to its original intention. Kisses exchanged beyond the firelight.

"It is as though some swift current of water swept you along with it."[3]

In Moravia, the small wooden house holds the memory of a daughter's feet on a bare floor, a daughter who waltzed out the door, with five small children, moved in the way a mother does, over the planks crossing the Lomná River, careful, careful – three steps, a foot lifted, the timing skewed as a child dropped a valise, another cried, and they danced a sweet sarabanda together toward Jablunkov, then Antwerp, then Canada. They never saw Horní Lomná again.

On the porch, almost deaf, aging feet find the tempo, slow, though the language she hears is not her own.

4. *Giga,* in Victoria, your final days

I can't keep up. My pulse races in the offices where we learn how quickly a life comes to its end. I hold your hand. Notes on a clipboard, blood pressure, the number of tumours gathered in a body. You refuse the treatments, remembering the needle through your chest wall, the first discovery of the malignant pleural effusion.

How quickly the years passed, how quickly we grew apart, too late the return, the counterpoint of our footwork, you holding my arm as we walked to the X-ray room, my boots brisk on the polished floor. Your chest on the screen made the technician come to me and say how sorry she was, how sorry. And you in the changing room, unable to lift your arms to put on your camisole, your scar uncovered, a vine of stitches like brambles covering where your breast had been, notes, notes on a long line, nicked with rests, yours, mine, how quickly the years do pass.

5. *Ciaccona*, first thing in the morning, a walk to Chesterman Beach

Move forward, linger, pause, advance the notes so perfectly timed, a bow of carbon, ebony, ivory, mother of pearl, abalone, bone, silk for the grip, advance, oh bow, lingering.

There are passages that find old sore places in my heart and remind them of the impact, the moment before the bruise. Yet how can that be? Notes, notes: inked marks on a five-line staff, one after another. A time signature. All of it an approximation, a correspondence, a calling to the page what is heard in the mind. I imagine his fingers playing the air, dipping a quill into ink, iron gall ink darkening to purple-black, a bruise in the quick ovals of the notes, the iron of it oxidizing on the paper and turning the notes brown. As a body turns to grey ash in the flame of cremation.

When the phone rang in the small hours and a nurse told me my mother had died, I felt punched, slammed in the chest and had to sit down on the carpet with the phone in my hand. I'd only tracked her down the evening before, a Sunday, and learned from a nurse that she'd been admitted to hospital the day before (we'd seen her the day before that) and wasn't expected to last the night. She danced toward me on a long beach.

A heart's anatomy: four chambers, two atria, right and left; two ventricles, left and right, and the wall that separates them. Her heart weakened as her lungs worked harder to pass the oxygenated blood back, harder as she gasped, found it difficult to manage the oxygen tank she never wanted, the rhythm fading, fading, one, two, gasp, her eyes fluttering. The wall that separated us, the dance slowing, slowing, the two-part pumping losing a rhythm she'd known all her (my) life. That I knew in utero and must find now.

It is the counterpoint of the self, the pulse that guides us through our days, left, right, the rhythm strong, then fading, the composer arriving home to learn that his beloved wife had died, was buried. "On one stave, for a small instrument, the man writes a whole world of the deepest thoughts and most powerful feelings."[4] His sorrow ours for the time it takes to draw notes out of sixty-four bars, twenty-nine variations on four strings, taking us to the end of time. Pernambuco, abalone, ivory, bone. As my grandmother walked, slow, with her children, one a baby wrapped in a shawl, in the snow on the road away from the village forever.

Or, first thing in the morning, a walk to Chesterman Beach, which was almost empty except for a few early risers with their joyous dogs. Mist, two huge ravens muttering and poking in the flotsam. *I'd been thinking a great deal about geographical loneliness.*

The others arrive. We, a family of twenty-nine, gather later on the beach, gather as I remove my parents' ashes from the bags within boxes and mix a scoop of each into Ziploc bags for those who want to take a portion to other places – a grove of trees, a hill, the corner of a room. Then a scoop of each, cinders and bone fragments, into an ice cream bucket for each family – mine, my brothers' – to take down the beach as a group, to say what they needed to say.

There are seven in my own group. We go to the water's edge and I tell my parents I loved them. I love them now, in the eyes and legs and hands of my children, from them, from each (my own cheekbones), and wish them peace. I bend down and let the waves wash into the bucket and out, two times, three times, as we all cry, watching what remains of them join the water, some of their bone fragments sinking into the wet sand, shining as mica shines, as the waves retreat, to be taken by crabs or clams or a rough-throated raven. And we retreat, too, back along the track we had made to the water, in slow time, a long harmonic progression, some of us holding hands, arms around my shoulders as I weep, slow, slow, the bass line underlying all the voices, our voices, entwined, each with a different version of their story, stories, triple time, slowed to the beat a heart makes from birth to death, expanding, contracting more than 3.5 billion times, as these tides rise and fall, 122,640 times, a life expanding and contracting, rising and falling, and we are flotsam on this long beach. We are the sweet notes of the violin, fingers stopping, finding the sorrow in the gut strings, the metal wound strings, steel, aluminum, gold; we are the string to their bow, hair from the tails of Siberian, Polish, Mongolian horses, raised in cold climates and strong. Black hairs more grabby, pale hairs more silken. Slow, the stroking of hairs across strings, my mother's hand on my head in sickness, in distress. My hand on her head that final day, sparse hair springy under my palm.

We are still here, though the warheads have been mentioned, the fury of retaliation. Though hurricanes whirl across the planet, rivers flood and wildfires burn entire towns. On a long beach I have put my mother and father into the tide. I am still here, though plastics fill our oceans and rivers break their dams. A violin, the last bars. Slow, slow, the return to a fire, the embrace of those who remain.

NOTES

1 John Berger, "Le Pont d'Arc," *Here is Where We Meet* (New York: Pantheon Books, 2005).

2 Johann Mattheson, *Der vollkommene Capellmeister* (Michigan: UMI Research Press, 1981).

3 Virginia Woolf, "A Dance at Queen's Gate," *A Passionate Apprentice: The Early Journals, 1897–1909* (Boston: Houghton Mifflin Harcourt, 1992).

4 Johannes Brahms, *Letters of Clara Schumann and Johannes Brahms, 1853–1896*, 2 vols., edited by Berthold Litzmann (Westport, CT: Hyperion Press, 1979).

MOM, I'M OKAY

Daniel Zomparelli

I'm writing this the day after the six-year anniversary of my mother's death. She died from a very rare disease after only a short year of health deterioration. Her death was both a surprise and not a surprise if you were looking at the situation from a distance.

I was twenty-five at the time, and if you skipped exactly a year back from her death, you would find me at the hospital being picked up by my mother. We are in Burnaby, BC, and I had just had my first panic attack. I was at home alone and I became dizzy and felt as if I would stop breathing. I called my mother, told her I was going to the hospital and she rushed over.

The first person at the hospital asked to take my heart rate; she said I appeared perfectly fine and asked if I had ever had a history of anxiety in my family. I laughed. My father and my sister were both on anxiety medication.

Months later, as my mother's heart deteriorated, my mother asked me if I would consider a train trip or a cruise to Alaska. Her heart capacity was so low that she would never be allowed on a plane. Doctors were surprised she could function, but she was managing enough to walk. I told her I would love to train to Montreal or go to Alaska.

My mother used to take us travelling constantly, and at a very young age. We often went on family trips: Puerto Vallarta, Disneyland, Italy, Argentina. I remember when she passed, finding a list of places she would hope to go to. I thought about visiting these places, like some sort of romantic comedy to deal with my grief and loneliness, but I hate travelling. I prefer to be in one place for long periods of time.

I used to text my mother every moment I landed from a flight. I still, to this day, mentally note that I should let my mother know I landed safely. That mental note only takes a moment for me to remember that she is dead.

A year after her death, I landed in Puerto Vallarta. I felt uneasy. Travelling always makes me uneasy, so this wasn't a new feeling. When we passed the restaurants and markets I was familiar with, I felt a tightness in my stomach. By the time we arrived at our small beachfront rental, I was having trouble breathing. I left my friends and sat on the beach for an hour doing my breathing exercises. This is where I first encountered the reality/fact that my grief was a world traveller.

When I was nine, I went to Italy with my father. We stayed for several months. I wouldn't realize until later that the vacation was a way for my parents to be apart. The moment we arrived at my zia's apartment, I had a nap. I woke up crying uncontrollably. I was without my mother for the first time in my life and I didn't know when I would see her again.

*

My sister Tina died when I was very young. The death of my sister split us all in half. It turned my mother distant. It made my father disappear into the living room couch.

When I was engaged to be married, my now husband and I were out for drinks. A few friends wanted to celebrate our engagement. We drank into the evening and a friend of mine, who also had lost his mother, gently noted that the wedding would be hard without my mother. That I should prepare for it, so that it isn't so overwhelming.

That night, I cried in front of my partner and told him that I could feel the constellation of loss, between my lost mother, my lost sister and all the pain between. I couldn't quite explain it, but I could feel the dots connecting and it was overwhelming.

"Mom, I landed safely."

In the middle of the ocean, on a cruise, my sister told me how she had been left alone so much. How after my eldest sister died, my mother crumbled, my father disappeared. She told me that she was looking for her pants for school but there were no clean clothes. She begged my mom for clean clothes and my mother replied with, "I'm sorry, I just can't do anything."

"She said she was okay," my sister explained. "She was hit by a car, and then she said she was okay." My mother took my sister Julia out to see my eldest sister Tina as she walked back to our Burnaby home. She was struck by a car as she crossed the street. My mother ran out and Tina got up from the street and said, "Mom, I'm okay." They took her in the ambulance and she died before she made it to the hospital.

Our backyard was mostly cement. Hard, unyielding cement. There were so many cracks in the cement, I would trace them to their original breaking point. Each broken space leading into two more and two more until it was a tree branch of crumbled cement.

When I was young, I used to throw water balloons at the cars in front of my house. One time a balloon connected and a car almost spun out and crashed. I ran behind my home as the driver knocked at our door and asked if a young brown-haired boy lived here. My mother said no.

Mom, I'm okay.

When my mom died, I went through the boxes of Tina's stuff. Found her diaries and her notes to boys. She had best friends and she had enemies and she had a crush. Something that gets washed away in death is all the small details. My mother's box of Tina's personal items felt like two stars connecting in the night's sky.

Six months ago, I had my wedding. It was small and in Los Angeles. A city my mother took me to twice. I even recently went to Disneyland, where every ride reminded me of when she took us there.

My friend was right. A lot of moments in the wedding I felt the weight of my mother missing. But it wasn't a new feeling. It felt like most moments of a sister missing. After it all, I was stuck in the United States for months until given a travel pass by the government (keeping the tradition of immigrants in my family). The moment I received my travel pass, my first thought was that I can see my mom again. My memory usually fails me when I'm away. Burnaby is where my mother resided. My mother is dead. Both these things are true.

*

Six years later, I still instinctively pick up my cell phone to text my mother, I'm okay.

I have since returned to Puerto Vallarta. My anxiety is at half of what it used to be going there. I used to resent going there because it meant weeks of being stuck with my family. Something I no longer resent now that I have come out of the closet to the majority of them.

I have not returned yet to Italy. A space I worry will trigger my anxiety to an unmanageable level. We continue to put off a family visit.

I return to Burnaby often, still going through the drawers and dressers of the home, desperately trying to find a new piece of my mother I might have missed.

We're now settling into our home in Los Angeles, and slowly I have been bringing bits and pieces of the memories of my mother and Tina to our home. It's a new challenge, being so far away from Burnaby, feeling like a memory lives at a specific address from which I am no longer a short drive from.

Travelling always brought out my worst anxiety because I used to think of all the terrible things that could happen while I was gone. That I could lose my family or friends when I wasn't looking. My mother hated me being at a geographical distance. She begged me not to move out after university and always insisted I text the moment I landed in any far-off place. I kept a lot of the anxieties associated with that, but I learned that it's all part of a constellation. It might be far from here, but it's all connected. I can see this now that it's a little further away.

NEVER RELEASED: HAMILTON, ON, AND SCOTCH VILLAGE, NS

Ben Gallagher

Released from history, here are some facts: on the evening of October 30, 2013, the air in Hamilton was cool. A man whose name I refuse to remember drank through the afternoon then got into a car. He wove his way down the Wentworth access road too quickly in the grey dusk. Too fast the car killed my partner as she jogged across the road. At our apartment I turned down the stew, wondered why she was running for so long, worried. Eventually I circled the block, uncertainty chewing away inside me, until I found a line of caution tape and entered an uncertainty so vast it swallows years.

I needed him to be without causes, so at first when I thought of him, he was a lightning bolt or a tidal wave. Without causes, I didn't have to be angry. Without causes, I didn't have to consider forgiveness. Without causes, nothing can be changed. This became the heart of my reaction – there was no response or information that could alter Zoë's death, so any attempt to lessen, shift, clarify or reconcile her loss felt fake. I pushed back at comfort, at excuses, at understanding. They just didn't matter. I wanted to sit at the bedrock of my sorrow, which was nothing less than the absurd and un-explainable movement from existence to absence.

Yet we are never released from history. Over these three years I have slowly allowed the past back in, seeing the ways in which my small grief is connected to much larger ones. Grief over the history of my culture: a culture where the cheapest, legal, shame-free medication is alcohol. A culture where the easiest, most encouraged and glorified way of moving is in a car. A culture where the fundamental unit of power and responsibility is the isolated individual. And in Canada, a culture that has been shaped by the stealing and subsequent destruction of Indigenous land.

Even if we are not released from this history, it is still a history that often goes denied.

> It's hard to unhook the heavy marble Nature from the
> chain around yr neck when history is stolen like
> water
> (Tommy Pico, *Nature Poem*)

Fuck this system, let's burn it all down, I say to myself sometimes.

Zoë died on Haudenosaunee land, but she grew up on the unceded territory of the Mi'kmaq in Halifax. In her twenties, she became part of a land co-op, five strangers who decided to join their lives together and enter into a relationship with the land and water of Scotch Village, Nova Scotia. After her death, I inherited her shares in the co-op and her entanglement with the land as well.

This means inheriting Western assumptions about property, such as the misguided and damaging notion that land can be owned. It means inheriting the ways in which this assumption about ownership has been used to accumulate wealth for me and my ancestors. It means inheriting the colonial history of Scotch Village, full of ongoing racism and linked not just to violence and broken treaties with the Mi'kmaq but also shipbuilding for the transatlantic slave trade, the expulsion of Acadians and the resettlement by New England Planters. It means inheriting rising sea levels that will eventually engulf the old Acadian dykes and sweep away Scotch Village, perhaps fuelled by environmentally destructive companies like Alton Gas who are currently investing in natural gas storage projects on the Sipekne'katik River that runs nearby.

Indigenous feminist Mishuana Goeman describes how settlers use maps and stories to read the landscape as empty. That emptiness then means the land can be owned, controlled and divided. For Goeman, Indigenous poetry is a way of remapping landscapes, filling them back up with the relationships that maps deny. Poetry can simultaneously express the history and ongoing presence of people within a landscape, so that Indigenous poetry produces "a new kind of spatial politics" where geographical imaginations are expanded.

> Indian land was far away in another world, across
>   state lines where grandparents plant corn and
>   herd sheep on a brown-eyed/blue-eyed horse . . .
>
> I always forget L.A. has sacred mountains.
> (Esther G. Belin, "Directional Memory")

Belin, like Pico, uses poetry to undo the artificial divide between rural wilderness and urban civilization – a divide that erases urban Indigenous presence. As Goeman makes clear, "Native stories speak to a storied land and storied peoples, connecting generations to particular locales and in a web of relationships." These stories contain alternative visions of both space and time, as they are experienced on the land and water, than those stories and visions put forward by a linear story of "progress," Western property law, nation-state borders or the abstract "environment."

In the months after her death, I walked the streets of Hamilton, screaming into the night. I spoke Zoë's name out loud, calling and calling. Eventually I realized that despite the fact that she died in Hamilton, she had begun a relationship to the place and people of Scotch Village. On some level it made sense that I would find her there rather than on a thin smear of asphalt.

When I moved to Scotch Village, I still howled, this time at a sky thick with stars. I placed my head in the tall grasses and spoke to her again. I gathered flowers from the field, found an abandoned robin's nest in the old crabapple tree, watched a raccoon skeleton get pounded clean in the rain. I gave myself over completely to grief, and as months passed, I realized I could find my way back toward my body and its daily hunger, need for sleep, its urge toward small joys.

Eve Tuck, in "Decolonization is Not A Metaphor," warns against and rejects what she calls "settler emplacement," the desire on the part of those of us not originally from this place to read ourselves into it and thus justify our presence. What does my individual grief mean, in the face of generations of grief over land that has been stolen? If I can sense Zoë's presence in this one small corner of a province, what must it be like to sense 14,000 years' worth of presence and have that be continually denied? However loud my grief is, I cannot allow it to cover this history that my grieving sits inside.

> I sit in the cool quiet office and invent myself some
>   laughs in an
> attempt to maneuver from a sticky kind of ancestral
>   sadness, bein a
> NDN person in occupied America, and the magic
>   often works
>
> until I think *why is it so damn hard to spell
>   maneuver* and *why does it
> always look wrong* my great grandparents had almost
>   no contact
> with white ppl like the shutter of a poem is the only
>   place where I can
> illusion myself some authority.
> (Tommy Pico, *Nature Poem*)

It would be so easy for me to believe that because I connect to Zoë through the land of Scotch Village, I have some claim to the place, or that she and the place claim me. It would be so easy to believe that because my grief is vast, it confers on me some power to speak about loss in general. When I walk through the fields gathering sweet fern or watching zipper spiders spin their elaborate webs, I let myself believe these easy feelings. But then I stand them up against Pico's ancestral sadness, against the illusory authority that generates my desire for emplacement, against the devastation that sits inside the very language in which I think and write, and I know that the easy feelings of my irreparable personal loss are not enough.

I am calling them easy feelings, it should be said, not because they are feelings that are easy to have. I am calling them easy because they are feelings my culture encourages me to have. And by having them and only them, I shut out other feelings that are even harder to reckon with. I am not told to feel that my sense of connection to this place comes at the expense of the people that place has been stolen from. That the magnitude of my personal loss is given legitimacy while the many losses suffered by Indigenous Peoples here are ignored, denied and erased. That I talk to others about my loss in the language of power, not in languages that have been actively suppressed. And that these losses are not commensurable with each other, are not an equalizing force, they do not clear the slate of history.

There must be some other way to talk and think and feel about grief.

Turning away, and turning toward. Even years after her death, I spend time in my mind in Hamilton. I swore I would never return to the city, but it, too, exerts a pull on me. And as I have expanded outwards from my concrete grieving rituals toward the larger grieving history of Canadian state violence, to the very largest grief of a dominant and destructive global culture, I've had to confront how my previous approach to an urban landscape also denied Indigenous presence.

This strange Western concept of "nature" and the "natural" is another violent border. It sits, alongside concepts like "normal," on the panel of judges that condemns grief that lasts too long, or any way of being and feeling that sits outside the acceptable range. The heavy marble Nature that weighs on Pico's urban NDN poetry, Belin's sacred skyscraper mountains collecting stardust, the histories and relationships and futures denied and yet thriving – when I maintain contact with the grieving place inside me I find it pulling me toward these landscapes as well.

Grief is what has provoked in me the desire to reckon with that history, and to commit myself to the protection and support of the land in Scotch Village. As James Baldwin writes, "The past is all that makes the present coherent, and . . . the past will remain horrible for exactly as long as we refuse to assess it honestly." The clarity and pain that comes with grief, for me at least, has become an opening and a provocation.

I return again to the rituals I began after Zoë's death, when I needed to find ways to be in contact with her. I had to acknowledge the truth of the emptiness her death was showing me, an emptiness that broke through the thin paper surface of the world around me. Speaking her name out loud. Sitting quiet in the grass. A lit candle, a photo, a collection of precious objects.

Being inside the immediacy of loss, and also being inside the long history of the places I am fortunate to live in, there is a kind of vibration that occurs. Perhaps it is the vibration between the individual and the structural, or between a human relationship to land and the land's relationship to humans. Whatever generates these feelings, I know I need both. I believe this is why rituals have come into my life and into my own writing.

> It is through our connection to
> ritual where the experience is
> horizontal, where we can imbibe

with everyone living and dead and
with people yet to be.

The poet Robert Desnos has a
line, "the living and the dead
give in and wave to me"

This is a place where poetry is
capable of taking us, a real
place where all of time is
suddenly present.
(CAConrad, "Poetry & Ritual")

Again, rituals and poetry allow us to see that places
contain both histories and futures, contain relationships
with the living and the dead. This requires a different kind of
language. It also requires breaking with a vision of the world
that sees everything as separate and individual, that believes
in ownership, that ignores the nurturing relationships around
us.

Now
make room in the mouth
for grassesgrassesgrasses
(Layli Long Soldier, *Whereas*)

Make room in the mouth for a place to speak through.
Make room in the mouth for the past and the many futures
that are held within every place. For me the beginning gestures
of making room began in Scotch Village, in the urge to
engage with the details of the natural world: feeling the water
coursing underground in spring, the dry seed pods scattering

in autumn, ice cracking on a winter river. And now that gesture has expanded back into cities, seeing that anywhere I find myself I can undertake rituals that make room for a place to thrive. That these rituals can be poems as well.

And as I write I think about the desire for resolution, for satisfaction, as another kind of emplacement. All the many nights I called out to Zoë and the stars, throwing myself into the darkness. How grief teaches me that I will live my whole life without satisfaction, desiring. That unresolved, unsatisfied and lost, still I can live. That my body, in place, through time, letting go, opening up, silent or speaking, knows how to be. That my body and language, much as I wish otherwise, are inescapably linked to destruction and violence. When experience becomes horizontal, and we work with language and poetry to express both loss and connection in terms that break from Western cultural values, the pressure for resolution lifts. At least for me, I keep slipping away from my culture's accessible version of sorrow and toward this uncomfortable vibration. While the vibration between my small sorrowing existence and larger sorrowful histories is unavoidable, incommensurable – I believe it is at the core of what grieving can teach.

WORKS CITED

Baldwin, James. *Notes of a Native Son*. Boston: Beacon Press, 1955.

Belin, Esther. *From the Belly of My Beauty*. Tucson: University of Arizona Press, 1999.

Conrad, CA. "Poetry & Ritual." *Literary Hub,* February 5, 2016. https://lithub.com/poetry-ritual/.

Goeman, Mishuana. *Mark My Words: Native Women Mapping Our Nations*. Minneapolis: University of Minnesota Press, 2013.

Long Soldier, Layli. *Whereas*. Minneapolis: Graywolf Press, 2017.

Pico, Tommy. *Nature Poem*. Portland: Tin House Books, 2017.

Tuck, Eve, and K. Wayne Yang. "Decolonization is Not a Metaphor." *Decolonization: Indigeneity, Education & Society* 1, no.1 (2012).

AUTHOR BIOGRAPHIES

KATHERINE BITNEY is the author of four books of poetry, a collection of essays on nature and the text for a choral piece. A fifth collection of poems is under construction. She has worked as editor, mentor, writing instructor and arts juror for over three decades. She lives, gardens and writes in Winnipeg.

ALICE BURDICK is the author of four full-length poetry collections, *Simple Master*, *Flutter*, *Holler* and *Book of Short Sentences*. *Deportment*, a book of selected poems, came out in 2018 from Wilfrid Laurier University Press. She has been a judge for various awards, including the bpNichol Chapbook Award and the Latner Writers' Trust Poetry Prize. She co-owns an independent bookstore in Lunenburg called Lexicon Books and now lives in Mahone Bay, Nova Scotia.

JENNA BUTLER is the author of three critically acclaimed books of poetry, *Seldom Seen Road*, *Wells* and *Aphelion*; a collection of ecological essays, *A Profession of Hope: Farming on the Edge of the Grizzly Trail*; and the Arctic travelogue *Magnetic North: Sea Voyage to Svalbard*. Her newest book, *Revery: A Year of Bees*, essays about women, beekeeping, trauma and climate grief, will be out with Wolsak and Wynn in 2020. A professor of creative writing and ecocriticism at Red Deer College, Butler lives in northern Alberta on an off-grid organic farm.

MARILYN DUMONT is of Cree/Métis ancestry. Poet, writer and professor, she teaches with the Faculty of Native Studies and the Department of English and Film Studies at the University of Alberta. Her four collections of poetry have all won either provincial or national poetry awards: *A Really Good Brown Girl* (1996), *green girl dreams Mountains* (2001), *that tongued belonging* (2007) and *The Pemmican Eaters* (2015). She was awarded the 2018 Lifetime Membership from the League of Canadian Poets for her contributions to poetry in Canada, and in 2019 was awarded the Alberta Lieutenant Governor's Distinguished Artist Award. She lives in Edmonton, AB.

BEN GALLAGHER is a poet, essayist and new father, currently in the middle of a PhD at the Ontario Institute for Studies in Education, researching non-linear pedagogy and poetic practices in community poetry workshops. Recent poems can be found in *untethered, Sewer Lid, The Puritan, (parenthetical)* and *Arc.* He lives in Lunenburg, NS.

CATHERINE GRAHAM's sixth poetry collection, *The Celery Forest*, was named a CBC Best Book of the Year and appears on their Ultimate Canadian Poetry list. Her debut novel, *Quarry*, won an Independent Publisher Book Awards gold medal for fiction, "The Very Best!" Book Awards for Best Fiction and was a finalist for the Sarton Women's Book Award for Contemporary Fiction and the Fred Kerner Book Award. *Æther: an out-of-body lyric* appears in 2020 with Wolsak and Wynn/Buckrider Books. She lives in Toronto.

CATHERINE GREENWOOD has lived and worked in British Columbia, New Brunswick, China and southeast England. Previous job titles include publications analyst, foreign expert, financial aid adjudicator and pet sitter. She has published two collections of poetry, *The Pearl King and Other Poems* and *The Lost Letters*. Her writing has appeared in many literary journals and anthologies, and has been recognized with several prizes, including a National Magazine Gold Award. She now lives in South Yorkshire where, as a PhD candidate at the University of Sheffield, she is pursuing an interest in Scottish Gothic poetry.

JANE EATON HAMILTON is the queer, non-binary, disabled author of nine books of creative non-fiction, memoir, fiction and poetry, including the 2016 novel *Weekend*, and two prior collections of short fiction. Their memoir was one of the UK *Guardian's* Best Books of the Year and a *Sunday Times* bestseller. They are the two-time winner of Canada's CBC Literary Award for fiction (2003/2014). They have had a Notable in BASS and three in BAE (2016/2018/2019) and have appeared in *The Journey Prize*, *Best Canadian Short Stories* and *Best Canadian Poetry*. They live near Vancouver, BC.

RICHARD HARRISON is the author of seven books of poetry, including the Governor General's Award–winning *On Not Losing My Father's Ashes in the Flood*. He teaches English and Creative Writing at Mount Royal University in Calgary, where he lives with his wife, Lisa.

DAVID HASKINS wanted to write ever since Enid Blyton sent him a handwritten postcard when he was seven. He also wanted to become a veterinary surgeon. He settled for mentorships under CanLit's A-listers Joe Rosenblatt, Austin Clarke, Matt Cohen, John Herbert, P.K. Page and others, and a career teaching English to high schoolers. His poetry books, *Reclamation* (Borealis, 1980) and *Blood Rises* (Guernica, 2020), and his literary memoir *This House Is Condemned* (Wolsak and Wynn, 2013) top a long list of published works that have won first place awards from the CBC, the Ontario Poetry Society, the Canadian Authors Association, gritLIT and Arts Hamilton. He continues to live in the family home in Grimsby, Ontario.

STEVEN HEIGHTON'S most recent books are a novel, *The Nightingale Won't Let You Sleep*, and a poetry collection, *The Waking Comes Late*, which received the 2016 Governor General's Award for Poetry. His short fiction and poetry have received four gold National Magazine Awards and have appeared in the *London Review of Books, Poetry Magazine* (Chicago), *Tin House, Best American Poetry, The Literary Review, Agni, Zoetrope, Geist* and five editions of *Best Canadian Stories*. In 2020, he will publish two books, *Reaching Mithymna* – a non-fiction account of the Middle Eastern refugee influx on Lesvos, Greece – and a children's book drawing on the same events. Heighton is also a translator, an occasional teacher and a reviewer for the *New York Times Book Review*. He has been based in Kingston, Ontario, for thirty years.

THERESA KISHKAN lives on the Sechelt Peninsula with her husband, John Pass, in a house she and John built and where they raised their children. She has published fourteen books, most recently *Euclid's Orchard*, a collection of essays about family history, botany, mathematics and love (Mother Tongue Publishing, 2017). Her novella, *The Weight of the Heart*, is due out from Palimpsest Press in spring 2020.

CHRISTINE LOWTHER is the author of several books (memoir and poetry) and co-editor of two anthologies. She won the inaugural Rainy Coast Arts Award for Significant Accomplishment from the Pacific Rim Arts Society. Her work appears in collections like *Rising Tides*, *Sweet Water*, *Force Field* and *Canadian Ginger*. Chris now lives in Tla-o-qui-aht unceded territory.

CANISIA LUBRIN is a writer, editor, critic and teacher from St. Lucia, published and anthologized internationally with translations of her work into Spanish, Italian and forthcoming in French and German. Her poetry debut *Voodoo Hypothesis* (Buckrider Books, 2017) was named a CBC Best Book and garnered multiple award nominations. *The Dyzgraphxst* (M&S, 2020) is her sophomore book of poetry. She holds an MFA from the University of Guelph and lives in Ontario.

ALICE MAJOR has published eleven books of poetry and a prize-winning collection of essays, *Intersecting Sets: A Poet Looks at Science*. Recent awards include the Lieutenant Governor of Alberta Distinguished Artist Award and an honorary doctorate from the University of Alberta. She served as Edmonton's first poet laureate, a city where she continues to live.

CATHERINE OWEN is the author of fifteen collections of poetry and prose, most recently *Riven* (ECW, 2020). Her work has been nominated for awards and won the Alberta Book Prize in 2010 for *Frenzy*. Along with this volume, she has also edited the anthology *The Other 23 and a Half Hours: Or Everything You Wanted to Know that Your MFA Didn't Teach You* (Wolsak & Wynn, 2015). She works in film props and writes book reviews at her Marrow blog at Wordpress.com. Born and raised in Vancouver, BC, she now lives in Edmonton, AB, again, this time in her 1905 house called Delilah.

JAMES PICARD has exhibited extensively in close to two hundred art exhibitions throughout North America and Europe, and next to world-renowned art legends such as Picasso, Matisse, Miró, and Warhol. He has also taught at several universities and has released three books on his art. He was the first artist to exhibit his paintings at the historical Alcatraz Prison in San Francisco, part of his *The Dark & The Wounded* painting series and world art tour, which he filmed and turned into a documentary film that won awards across the North American film festival circuit in 2017/18, culminating in a screening in May 2018 at the 71st Cannes International Film Festival in France. He currently resides in California.

NIKKI REIMER writes poetry, non-fiction and micro-reviews, and dabbles in art. Published books are *My Heart is a Rose Manhattan* (Talon Books, 2019), *DOWNVERSE* (Talon Books, 2014) and *[sic]* (Frontenac House, 2010). She continues to live in Calgary, AB, on the traditional territories of the people of Treaty 7.

WAUBGESHIG RICE is an author and journalist from Wasauksing First Nation on Georgian Bay. His first short story collection, *Midnight Sweatlodge*, was inspired by his experiences growing up in an Anishinaabe community, and won an Independent Publishers Book Award in 2012. His debut novel, *Legacy*, followed in 2014. A French translation of *Legacy* was published in 2017. His latest novel, *Moon of the Crusted Snow*, was released in 2018 and quickly became a bestseller. He presently lives in Sudbury, Ontario, with his wife and son.

LISA RICHTER is the author of a book of poetry, *Closer to Where We Began* (Tightrope Books, 2017). Her work has previously appeared in *The New Quarterly*, *CV2*, *The Puritan*, *The Malahat Review*, *Literary Review of Canada* and the anthology *Jack Layton: Art in Action* (Quattro Books, 2013). Her next collection of poems, *Nautilus and Bone*, is forthcoming with Frontenac House in fall 2020. She lives in Toronto.

LYNN TAIT is a Toronto-born poet/photographer. Her poems have appeared in various literary journals including *Vallum*, *FreeFall*, and in over one hundred anthologies. She's also published a chapbook and co-authored a book with four other poets. She currently resides in Sarnia, Ontario.

SHARON THESEN has been living, working, teaching and writing in British Columbia, from Kamloops to Prince George to Vancouver (for a long while), and more recently in the Okanagan Valley. A poet, editor and critic, she is Professor Emeritus of Creative Writing at UBC's Okanagan campus.

ONJANA YAWNGHWE is the author of two books of poetry, *Fragments, Desire* (Oolichan, 2017) and *The Small Way* (Caitlin, 2018). She recently illustrated the novel *Little Blue Encyclopedia (for Vivian)* by Hazel Jane Plante and has illustrations forthcoming in *The Broken Boat* by Daniela Elza. She is currently working on a graphic novel about her family and Myanmar (Burma). She still lives in Coquitlam, BC.

DANIEL ZOMPARELLI is the author of *Davie Street Translations* (Talonbooks), and *Rom Com* (Talonbooks) co-written with Dina Del Bucchia. His first collection of short stories, *Everything Is Awful and You're a Terrible Person* (Arsenal Pulp Press), was nominated for the 2018 Ethel Wilson Fiction Prize. He is an executive producer and host of the podcast *I'm Afraid That*, produced with Little Everywhere. He lives in Los Angeles.

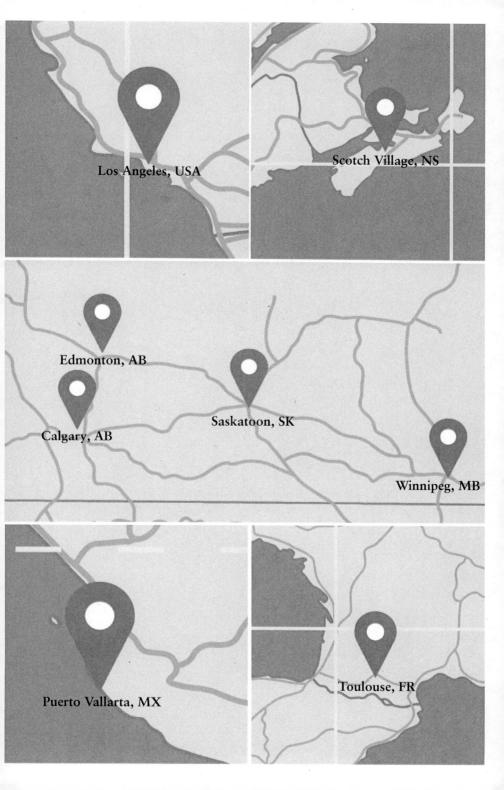

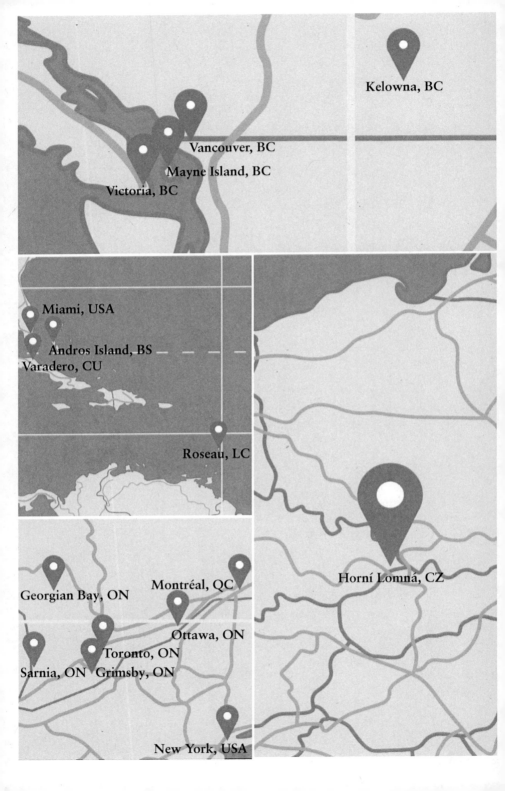